PISA

Travel Guide

Comprehensive Guide Exploring Tuscany's Top Attractions, Expert Local Advice, and Best Activities With A Detailed Itinerary.

RICKSON MICHAEL

Copyright © 2025 Rickson Michael. All rights reserved.

Thankful to you for consenting to protected innovation guidelines by downloading this book through genuine methods and by not replicating, checking, or spreading any piece of this book.

The Ultimate Guide to Explore Pisa Like Local & Everything you need To Explore Tuscany's Top Attractions.

Welcome to Pisa, where every day feels like a celebration.

TABLE OF CONTENTS

WELCOME TO PISA 9

CHAPTER 1 15

OVERVIEW PISA 16

    History of Pisa 16

    Culture of Pisa 18

    Geography & Topography of Pisa 27

CHAPTER 2 31

TRAVEL SMART 32

    What You Need To Know Before Traveling to Pisa 32

    Getting to Pisa 37

    Getting Around Pisa 40

    Weather and Best Time to Visit 43

    Pisa on a Budget & Travel Tips 45

CHAPTER 3 50

PISA TOP ATTRACTIONS 50

    Marina di Pisa Beach 51

    Tirrenia Beach 52

    Marina di Vecchiano Beach 52

    Calambrone Beach 53

    The Leaning Tower of Pisa 54

    Cathedral of Santa Maria Assunta 55

    Baptistery 57

    Campo Santo (Sacred Field) 58

    Museo dell'Opera del Duomo (Cathedral Museum) 59

    Murale Tuttomondo by Keith Haring 60

    Arsenals & Museum of Ancient Ships 61

    Santa Maria della Spina 62

    Borgo Stretto 63

    Palazzo dei Cavalieri 64

Palazzo Blu 65

Basilica Romanica di San Piero a Grado 65

Orto Botanico (Botanic Garden) 66

Santo Stefano dei Cavalieri 67

Piazza delle Gondole 68

Museo Nazionale di San Matteo (National Museum of San Matteo)
.... 69

CHAPTER 4 71

5-DAY ITINERARIES IN PISA 71

CHAPTER 5 81

RESTAURANT RECOMMENDATION 81

CHAPTER 6 87

HOTELS RECOMMENDATION 87

CHAPTER 7 93

NIGHTLIFE AND SHOPPING 93

Nightlife in Pisa 93

Shopping in Pisa 97

CHAPTER 8 101

DAY TRIPS FROM PISA.. 102

Cinque Terre... 102

Lucca... 111

Florence 119

Siena.. 141

Rome 157

CHAPTER 9 191

TRAVEL RESOURCES FOR PISA 191

Travel Phrases... 191

Tourist Information Centers 195

Emergency Contacts.. 197

CONCLUSION.. 199

WELCOME TO PISA

It is my pleasure to guide you through this enchanting city with my latest travel book. Having explored various corners of the world as a travel guidebook author, I bring a wealth of experience and a deep passion for uncovering hidden gems and sharing them with fellow adventurers. My travels have given me a unique perspective on the world, allowing me to appreciate both the well-known landmarks and the lesser-known treasures that each location has to offer. This extensive travel experience is what I bring to the table in every guidebook I write, ensuring that my readers have a rich and immersive experience.

My connection with Pisa goes beyond just a visit; it is a city that has fascinated me with its rich history, vibrant culture, and architectural marvels. From the iconic Leaning Tower to the tranquil Arno River, Pisa offers a diverse range of attractions that cater to all kinds of travelers. This book is a culmination of my in-depth exploration of the city, aiming to provide you with a comprehensive guide that goes beyond the typical tourist experience.

In an age where information is readily available online, you might wonder why you should invest in a travel guidebook. The answer lies in the depth and reliability of the information you'll find within these pages. Unlike fleeting online articles or generic travel apps, this guidebook is a meticulously curated resource, offering you insights that are both comprehensive and specific to Pisa. It combines the latest information with timeless tips, ensuring you have a memorable and hassle-free trip.

This book is designed to be your ultimate companion in Pisa, providing you with everything you need to know to make the most of your visit. Here's a glimpse of what you can expect:

1. Historical Context: Understanding the history of Pisa is crucial to appreciating its present. This guide offers a detailed account of the city's evolution, from its origins in the Roman era to its significance during the Renaissance and beyond. You'll learn about the pivotal events and influential figures that shaped Pisa into the city it is today.
2. Architectural Marvels: Pisa is renowned for its architectural wonders, most notably the Leaning Tower. But the city's architectural heritage goes beyond this iconic landmark. The book provides in-depth information about other significant structures such as the Pisa Cathedral, the Baptistery, and various historic

churches and palaces. Each entry includes detailed descriptions, historical backgrounds, and practical information for visitors.

3. Cultural Insights* To truly experience Pisa, one must immerse themselves in its culture. This guide delves into the local customs, traditions, and festivals that make Pisa unique. Whether it's the lively celebrations of Luminara or the historical reenactments during the Gioco del Ponte, you'll find a wealth of information to help you connect with the local culture.

4. Practical Tips: Traveling can sometimes be challenging, especially in a foreign city. This book is packed with practical tips to make your journey smoother. From navigating public transportation to finding the best local eateries, you'll have all the information you need at your fingertips. There are also sections dedicated to accommodations, shopping, and safety tips to ensure you have a worry-free trip.

The city's calendar is dotted with festivals and events that offer a glimpse into its rich cultural tapestry. Whether you're visiting during the vibrant Luminara festival in June, where the city is illuminated by thousands of candles, or the historic Regata di

San Ranieri, a traditional boat race on the Arno River, there is always something happening in Pisa.

During your holiday in Pisa, you'll experience the city's warm hospitality and lively atmosphere. The locals, known for their friendly and welcoming nature, add to the charm of the city. Stroll through the bustling streets, enjoy a gelato by the river, or simply relax in one of the many piazzas as you soak in the vibrant ambiance.

Pisa is not just about sightseeing; it's about experiencing life the Pisan way. Take a leisurely walk through the medieval streets, sample the delicious Tuscan cuisine, and immerse yourself in the local culture. Whether you're an art enthusiast, a history buff, or a foodie, Pisa has something for everyone.

In this guidebook, you'll find everything you need to make your trip to Pisa unforgettable. From detailed historical insights to practical travel tips, I've covered all aspects to ensure you have a well-rounded and enriching experience. This book is more than just a guide; it's a companion that will help you navigate the city with ease and uncover its many treasures.

So, whether you're planning your first trip to Pisa or returning to explore more of its wonders, this guidebook is your key to a memorable adventure. Dive in, and let Pisa enchant you with its beauty, history, and charm.

Thank you for choosing this guidebook. Here's to an incredible journey in Pisa!

CHAPTER 1
OVERVIEW PISA

History of Pisa

Pisa's history is a fascinating tapestry woven from centuries of cultural, economic, and political developments. Situated along the Arno River, Pisa rose to prominence in the medieval era, becoming one of the most powerful maritime republics in Italy. Its strategic location and robust naval fleet allowed Pisa to dominate Mediterranean trade routes and establish colonies across the Mediterranean and Black Sea regions. This era of prosperity and power, from the 11th to the 13th centuries, saw the construction of some of Pisa's most iconic structures, including the famous Leaning Tower, the Cathedral, and the Baptistery, all located in the Piazza dei Miracoli.

During the 12th century, Pisa's naval prowess was at its peak, evidenced by significant victories such as the conquest of the Balearic Islands and the defeat of the Saracens.

However, the 13th century brought challenges, notably the Battle of Meloria in 1284, where Pisa suffered a crushing defeat at the hands of its rival Genoa. This loss marked the beginning of Pisa's decline as a maritime power. The city's fortunes further waned in the 14th century due to internal strife, the Black Death, and continued pressure from rival city-states.

By the late 14th century, Pisa fell under the control of the Florentine Republic, marking the end of its independence. Despite this political shift, Pisa continued to be a significant cultural and intellectual hub. The University of Pisa, founded in 1343, attracted scholars from across Europe and played a crucial role in the Renaissance. It remains one of Italy's premier institutions of higher learning.

The Renaissance period brought a renewed interest in art and science to Pisa. The city became a center of learning and innovation, with notable figures such as Galileo Galilei, who was born in Pisa in 1564, contributing to its intellectual legacy. Galileo's work in astronomy, physics, and mathematics had a profound impact on the scientific revolution.

In the 19th century, Pisa, like much of Italy, experienced significant political upheaval. The unification of Italy in the 1860s brought Pisa into the newly established Kingdom of Italy. During this period, the city underwent modernization and expansion, integrating more closely with the broader Italian state.

The 20th century saw Pisa face the trials of both World Wars. The city suffered considerable damage during World War II, particularly from Allied bombings. Post-war reconstruction efforts restored much of Pisa's historical architecture, preserving its rich heritage for future generations. The latter half of the 20th century and the early 21st century have seen Pisa emerge as a major tourist destination, renowned for its architectural marvels and vibrant cultural scene.

Today, Pisa seamlessly blends its illustrious past with a modern, dynamic present. The city continues to attract millions of visitors annually, drawn by its historical landmarks, academic excellence, and the enduring charm of its medieval streets. Whether wandering through the ancient squares or exploring the bustling markets, visitors to Pisa can feel the weight of history at every turn, making it a truly enriching travel experience.

Culture of Pisa

Pisa's culture is a vibrant tapestry reflecting centuries of history, artistic achievement, and regional pride. Nestled in the heart of Tuscany, Pisa embodies the quintessential Italian spirit, offering a unique blend of tradition and modernity that captivates visitors from around the globe.

The people of Pisa, known as Pisans, are renowned for their warmth, hospitality, and strong sense of local identity.

The city, with its population of around 90,000, is home to a mix of lifelong residents and a dynamic student community, thanks to the prestigious University of Pisa. Italian is the primary language spoken here, with a distinct Tuscan accent that adds a melodic quality to the speech. While many locals speak English, especially in tourist areas, learning a few basic Italian phrases can enrich your experience and endear you to the residents.

Pisan cuisine is a delightful expression of Tuscan culinary traditions, characterized by simplicity, fresh ingredients, and robust flavors. The local diet prominently features olive oil, bread, pasta, and a variety of meats and cheeses. Traditional dishes to try include Cecina, a savory chickpea flour pancake, and Baccalà alla Pisana, a flavorful salt cod stew. Seafood lovers will relish the fresh catches from the nearby Ligurian Sea, often served grilled or in rich, tomato-based sauces.

No meal is complete without sampling the local wines. Tuscany is famous for its wine production, and Pisa is no exception. Enjoy a glass of Chianti or Vernaccia di San Gimignano, paired perfectly with your meal. For those with a sweet tooth, the Vin Santo, a dessert wine, is traditionally served with Cantucci (almond biscuits) for dipping.

Music and dance are integral parts of Pisan culture, with influences ranging from medieval chants to contemporary tunes. The city hosts various music festivals throughout the year, celebrating genres from classical to jazz. Traditional Tuscan folk music, characterized by the use of instruments like the accordion and mandolin, is often accompanied by lively dances such as the "Saltarello" and "Pizzica". These cultural expressions are most vividly experienced during local festivals and events, where the streets come alive with performances and communal dancing.

Pisa's artistic heritage is illustrious, with the city playing a significant role during the Italian Renaissance. The city's architecture, from the Leaning Tower to the intricate facades of churches, stands as a testament to its rich artistic past. Today, Pisa continues to nurture its arts scene with numerous galleries, museums, and workshops.

Local crafts are deeply rooted in tradition, with artisans producing exquisite ceramics, leather goods, and jewelry. The Piazza dei Miracoli and surrounding areas offer a plethora of shops where you can find handmade souvenirs. Additionally, the Antiques Market in Piazza dei Cavalieri, held monthly, is a treasure trove for those interested in vintage and handcrafted items.

Pisa, renowned for its iconic Leaning Tower, is also a city rich in local customs and traditions that provide visitors with a deep sense of its cultural identity. Understanding and respecting these customs will enhance your experience and help you connect more authentically with the locals.

Pisans, like many Italians, are known for their warmth and hospitality. Greetings are typically enthusiastic; a friendly "Ciao" or "Buongiorno" (good morning) accompanied by a smile is common. Among close acquaintances, it's customary to exchange two cheek kisses, starting with the right cheek. When addressing someone formally, use titles such as "Signore" (Mr.) or "Signora" (Mrs.) followed by their surname. Politeness is highly valued, so saying "Per favore" (please) and "Grazie" (thank you) is essential.

Meals in Pisa are leisurely affairs and are seen as an opportunity to enjoy food and company. Lunch, or Pranzo, is typically the main meal of the day, usually enjoyed between 12:30 and 2:30 PM. Dinner, or Cena, is served later, often starting around 8 PM.

It's polite to wait until everyone is served before beginning to eat and to keep your hands visible on the table, but not your elbows.

Tipping is appreciated but not obligatory; rounding up the bill or leaving a small amount is considered sufficient.

Italians, including Pisans, generally dress stylishly and take pride in their appearance. While casual attire is acceptable, especially for sightseeing, it's advisable to dress more formally when dining out or visiting religious sites. When entering churches, shoulders and knees should be covered out of respect. In summer, lightweight fabrics are preferable due to the warm climate, but keep in mind that evenings can be cooler.

Pisa's calendar is filled with vibrant festivals that reflect its rich cultural heritage. One of the most significant is the Luminara di San Ranieri, celebrated on June 16th in honor of the city's patron saint. The Arno River is illuminated with thousands of candles, creating a magical atmosphere. Another major event is the Gioco del Ponte (Game of the Bridge), held on the last Saturday of June.

This historical reenactment features teams from different neighborhoods competing in a tug-of-war on the city's main bridge.

When shopping in local markets, bargaining is not customary, and prices are generally fixed. However, in some tourist areas or with street vendors, there might be room for polite negotiation. Always greet shopkeepers with a "Buongiorno" or "Buonasera" (good evening) upon entering, and thank them with a "Grazie" when leaving, even if you haven't made a purchase.

Catholicism plays a significant role in the daily life of many Pisans. Respect for religious practices and sites is important. When visiting churches or attending mass, dress modestly and maintain a quiet demeanor. It's also polite to refrain from taking photographs during services. Many locals may cross themselves when passing a church or religious icon, a small gesture of reverence that visitors should be aware of.

Pisans take pride in their city's cleanliness and natural beauty. Littering is frowned upon, and there are strict regulations regarding waste disposal and recycling. Public spaces, including parks and historical sites, are well-maintained, and visitors are expected to treat them with respect. It's also important to be mindful of noise levels, especially in residential areas, to avoid disturbing the peace.

When using public transportation, such as buses or trains, it's customary to offer your seat to the elderly, pregnant women, or those with disabilities. Tickets must be purchased and validated before boarding, and failure to do so can result in fines. Taxis are widely available, but it's advisable to use official taxi services rather than accepting rides from unofficial drivers.

By embracing these local customs, you'll not only show respect for Pisan traditions but also gain a deeper appreciation for the city's cultural nuances.

Event and festivals

Luminara di San Ranieri

One of Pisa's most enchanting events is the Luminara di San Ranieri, held annually on June 16th in honor of the city's patron saint, San Ranieri. On this night, the city's buildings along the Arno River are adorned with over 70,000 candles, creating a breathtaking display of lights. The reflection of the candles on the water, combined with fireworks at the end of the evening, makes for a magical experience. This celebration dates back to

1688 and attracts both locals and tourists who gather to enjoy the illuminated spectacle, music, and street performances.

Gioco del Ponte

Another significant event is the Gioco del Ponte (Game of the Bridge), which takes place on the last Saturday of June. This historical reenactment dates back to medieval times and involves a ceremonial parade followed by a competitive battle between teams from different neighborhoods. The competition takes place on the Ponte di Mezzo, where participants dressed in traditional armor attempt to push a heavy cart to the opposing team's side.

Regata di San Ranieri

On June 17th, the day after the Luminara, the Regata di San Ranieri is held on the Arno River. This historic rowing race features four boats representing the city's ancient districts: Santa Maria, San Francesco, San Martino, and Sant'Antonio. The race commemorates Pisa's maritime history and is a highly anticipated event, with rowers dressed in traditional costumes. The competition is fierce, and the winning team earns not only victory but also honor for their district.

Pisa Book Festival

For literature enthusiasts, the Pisa Book Festival is an annual highlight. Typically held in November, this independent publishing fair showcases Italian and international authors, offering book signings, readings, and discussions. The festival provides a platform for emerging writers and a meeting point for book lovers.

Pisa Jazz Festival

Music lovers will appreciate the Pisa Jazz Festival, which runs throughout the year with a concentration of events in the summer months. This festival brings together renowned jazz musicians from Italy and around the world, hosting concerts in various venues across the city, including historic theaters and outdoor spaces. The festival enriches Pisa's cultural life and provides a delightful experience for jazz aficionados.

Antiques Market

Every second weekend of the month, except in July and August, Pisa hosts an Antiques Market in the historic Piazza dei Cavalieri and surrounding streets. This market is a treasure trove for collectors and those interested in vintage items, offering antiques, collectibles, artworks, and furniture. The market's lively atmosphere and the chance to discover unique pieces make it a must-visit for anyone in Pisa during these weekends.

Carnevale di Pisa

Though not as famous as the Carnivals of Venice or Viareggio, the Carnevale di Pisa is a festive event usually held in February or March. The carnival features parades, masquerades, and various public celebrations, with participants donning elaborate costumes and masks. It's a vibrant display of creativity and a fun-filled event for all ages, reflecting the playful side of Pisan culture.

Feast of Santa Caterina

In late April, Pisa celebrates the Feast of Santa Caterina, honoring Saint Catherine of Siena, the patroness of Italy. The celebration includes religious processions, special church services, and community gatherings.

Geography & Topography of Pisa

Pisa, located in the Tuscany region of central Italy, boasts a diverse and captivating geography that contributes to its unique charm and allure. The city is situated in the Arno River valley, approximately 10 kilometers (6 miles) from the Ligurian Sea.

This strategic location not only provides stunning river views but also places Pisa at a crossroads of historical trade routes and cultural exchange.

The Arno River, which flows through the heart of Pisa, has historically been a vital waterway for commerce and transport, shaping the city's development and prosperity. The riverbanks, lined with historic buildings and charming promenades, offer picturesque vistas and are ideal for leisurely strolls, especially at sunset when the light casts a golden hue over the city.

Pisa is part of the fertile coastal plain known as the Pisan Plain, which is bordered by the Apuan Alps to the north and the Pisan Mountains to the east. The Apuan Alps, with their rugged limestone peaks, are famous for their marble quarries, producing the high-quality marble used in many of Italy's renowned sculptures and buildings, including some structures in Pisa itself. These mountains provide a dramatic backdrop to the city and offer opportunities for hiking and exploration.

The Pisan Mountains, a smaller range, are rich in Mediterranean vegetation and dotted with ancient monasteries, castles, and quaint villages. Monte Pisano, the highest peak in this range, offers panoramic views of the surrounding countryside, the city of Pisa, and even the distant sea. The hills are crisscrossed with trails that are perfect for trekking and provide a tranquil escape from the urban bustle.

Pisa's proximity to the Ligurian Sea influences its climate, giving it mild, wet winters and hot, dry summers. The coastal environment also means that the city enjoys refreshing sea breezes, particularly welcome during the hotter months. Marina di Pisa, a nearby seaside resort, offers sandy beaches and clear waters, making it a popular destination for both locals and tourists looking to relax and enjoy the Mediterranean climate.

In terms of urban topography, Pisa is relatively flat, making it easy to navigate on foot or by bicycle, which is a popular mode of transportation among locals. The historic center of Pisa is characterized by narrow, winding streets and open squares, with the most famous being the Piazza dei Miracoli, home to the iconic Leaning Tower, the Cathedral, the Baptistery, and the Camposanto.

This UNESCO World Heritage Site is a testament to Pisa's architectural and cultural heritage, drawing visitors from around the world.

Beyond the historic center, Pisa features a mix of residential neighborhoods, green parks, and modern amenities, reflecting its role as both a historic city and a vibrant university town. The presence of the University of Pisa, one of the oldest universities in Europe, contributes to the dynamic and youthful atmosphere of the city.

CHAPTER 2
TRAVEL SMART

What You Need To Know Before Traveling to Pisa

Public Holidays

In Pisa, public holidays include:

- New Year's Day (January 1)
- Epiphany (January 6)
- Easter Sunday and Monday (variable dates)
- Liberation Day (April 25)
- Labour Day (May 1)
- Republic Day (June 2)
- Assumption Day (August 15)
- All Saints' Day (November 1)
- Immaculate Conception (December 8)
- Christmas Day (December 25)
- St. Stephen's Day (December 26)

On these days, government offices, banks, and many businesses are closed.

Healthcare

Italy has a high-quality healthcare system. EU citizens can use their European Health Insurance Card (EHIC) for medical services. Non-EU visitors should ensure they have travel insurance covering medical expenses.

Electricity

Electricity in Pisa is 230V, 50Hz. Plug types C, F, and L are used. Visitors from countries with different plug types will need an adaptor.

WiFi and Internet Access

WiFi is widely available in hotels, cafes, restaurants, and public places. Many establishments offer free WiFi, and there are also public WiFi hotspots in various locations around the city.

Visas

EU citizens do not need a visa to visit Italy. Visitors from other countries should check visa requirements before traveling. Schengen visas are applicable for those needing a visa.

Cell Phones

To use your phone in Pisa, ensure it is unlocked and compatible with GSM networks. SIM cards can be purchased at mobile phone shops and convenience stores. Major providers include TIM, Vodafone, and Wind Tre.

Plugs

Italy uses plug types C, F, and L. Ensure you have the appropriate adaptor if your devices use a different plug type.

Tipping

- Airport and Hotel Parking Attendants: €1-2 for assistance.
- Bartenders: Rounding up the bill or leaving small change.
- Hotel Maids: €1-2 per day.
- Parking Valets: €1-2.
- Restaurant Servers: Service charge is often included; if not, 10% is appreciated.
- Taxi Drivers: Rounding up the fare or adding a couple of euros.

Adaptors

Ensure you have an adaptor for plug types C, F, or L if your devices use a different plug type.

Opening Hours

- Restaurants: Generally open from 12:00-14:30 for lunch and 19:00-22:30 for dinner.
- Bars: Open from early morning until late at night, typically from 7:00 until 1:00 or later.
- Shops: Usually open from 9:00-13:00 and 15:30-19:30. Many shops close on Sunday.
- Banks: Open from 8:30-13:30 and 14:45-15:45, Monday to Friday. Closed on weekends and public holidays.
- Post Offices: Open from 8:30-13:30, Monday to Saturday. Closed on Sunday and public holidays.
- Hotels: Reception is typically open 24 hours a day, but check-in and check-out times vary.

Money

Pisa, like many other European cities, uses the Euro (€). Visitors unfamiliar with this currency should note that banknotes are available in denominations of 5, 10, 20, 50, 100, 200, and 500 euros, while coins are available in 1, 2, 5, 10, and 20 eurocents, as well as 1 and 2 euro coins.

Pisa offers numerous currency exchange options, with banks being the most recommended due to their favorable rates. Most banks are located in central Pisa. For example, the Cassa di Risparmio di Pisa has a branch at the Galileo Galilei Airport. Bank opening hours generally span from 08:30 AM to around 04:00 PM, with a lunch break from approximately 1:30 PM to 2:30 PM. Exchange desks are also available at major tourist spots such as the airport, bus and train stations, hotels, and restaurants, though their rates are typically less favorable than those offered by banks. Pisa is well-equipped with ATMs that accept a wide variety of cards. To avoid running out of cash, it is advisable to carry cards from well-known companies.

Communications and Internet

Almost all accommodation facilities in Pisa provide internet access, either via WiFi or wired connections. Additional internet access options include numerous internet cafes, shopping centers, and other tourism-related establishments. Post offices can be a useful alternative for certain communications or deliveries. The main post office in Pisa is located at Piazza Vittorio Emanuele II, 7, 9. Another convenient post office is situated in the arrivals hall of the terminal building at Galileo Galilei Airport.

The official language in Pisa is Italian. However, staff in most tourist establishments can communicate in English, and often in

German, French, and Spanish as well. Tourists with some knowledge of Italian will find it easier to navigate Pisa and its surroundings. Understanding Latin can also be helpful for reading inscriptions at many tourist sites.

Time Zone

Pisa operates on Central European Time (CET), which is GMT+1 hour.

Getting to Pisa

Traveling to Pisa by Plane

Flying is the most efficient way to reach Pisa. The city's air travel needs are served by Galileo Galilei International Airport, which connects Pisa to destinations across Italy and the world, thanks to the 18 airlines operating there. The airport's prime location, just 1 kilometer south of the city center and well-integrated with Tuscany's road and rail systems, makes it a key entry point to both Pisa and the region.

Arriving in Pisa by Train

Traveling to Pisa by train is a convenient option, connecting the city to several Tuscan destinations, including Florence, Livorno,

Siena, and Lucca, as well as major Italian cities like Rome and Genoa. Pisa's primary train stations are San Rossore Station, near Piazza del Duomo, and Pisa Central Station, with buses transporting passengers to the city center from both locations.

For those traveling from Lucca, the journey to Pisa takes approximately 30 minutes, with 24 trains running daily. Siena is about an hour away, serviced by hourly trains. The trip from Florence to Pisa takes about an hour and a half, with around 40 trains per day to meet the high demand. If you're traveling from Rome, expect a journey of about 3 hours, with 20 trains making the trip each day. For those not flying or driving, train travel offers an efficient and reliable alternative.

Traveling to Pisa by Bus

Exploring Tuscany via bus is a fantastic option, as buses offer the most economical mode of transport in Italy, even though trains are often seen as more efficient for land travel. Pisa is well-connected by numerous bus services linking it to major Italian and Tuscan cities.

Rome and Florence, in particular, have excellent bus connections to Pisa. Three main bus operators serve Pisa's tourist routes, each covering different destinations. Autolinee

Lazzi provides routes connecting Lucca and Viareggio to Pisa. CPT (Compagnia Pisana Trasporti) ensures reliable transportation between Pisa and the surrounding province. Additionally, CLAP operates regular routes to Lucca and Pietrasanta. The primary intercity bus station in Pisa is located at Piazza Vittorio Emanuele II, near the Central Station.

Driving to Pisa

Traveling to Pisa by car is highly recommended for those who enjoy the scenic beauty and tourist attractions of Tuscany. Italy's robust road infrastructure makes this journey convenient, though the complex network of motorways can be confusing for those unfamiliar with the routes. The primary road to Pisa is the SS1 Aurelia, which connects cities such as Florence, Rome, Bologna, and Genoa to Pisa. For travelers starting in Florence, the best route involves taking the A11 Florence-Mare Motorway or the Florence-Pisa-Livorno expressway before joining the SS1 Aurelia. Those coming from Genoa should travel on the A12 Genoa-Rosignano Motorway before merging onto the SS1 Aurelia. For visitors departing from Rome, the optimal route involves taking the A1 Motorway towards Florence, then following the A11 Motorway and SS1 Aurelia to reach Pisa.

Getting Around Pisa

Navigating Pisa by Car

Exploring Pisa and its province by car allows for a flexible and personalized experience. Whether you are using your own vehicle or renting one, cars provide the convenience of moving at your own pace. Car rentals are readily available at the International Galileo Galilei Airport in Pisa, where over ten car rental companies operate, including well-known brands such as Hertz, Avis, and Europcar.

However, it's crucial to be aware of the ZTL (Limited Traffic Zone) restrictions in Pisa's historic center. These areas are off-limits to non-resident vehicles, meaning only public transportation and authorized cars can access them. Violating these restrictions can result in hefty fines. Therefore, it's advisable to park your car outside these zones.

Despite the ZTL restrictions, Pisa offers numerous parking options. Free parking spaces can be found around the city, especially on the outskirts. Paid parking lots are also available and can be more convenient, especially if you want to be closer to the city center. The cost and availability of parking can vary, so it's beneficial to check local signage and parking meters for specific information.

Once you've parked, you can easily reach Pisa's historic center either by walking or using the local bus system. Walking allows you to enjoy the scenic beauty and charm of the city's streets, while buses provide a quick and efficient way to get to major attractions. The local bus network is well-organized, with frequent routes covering all key areas of Pisa.

Getting Around Pisa by Bus

Buses are a highly efficient way to navigate Pisa, providing convenient access to both the historic center and various parts of the city. The LAM Rossa bus line is particularly useful, connecting Pisa's airport and central station to the main attractions in the historic center. Bus tickets are easy to purchase, as all buses are equipped with ticket machines onboard. For more information on routes and schedules, you can visit the official website of Pisa's public transport provider, Pisa Mobilità, at [pisamobilita.it](http://www.pisamobilita.it).

Exploring Pisa by Motorcycle

Motorcycles offer a flexible alternative to cars for getting around Pisa, free from the restrictions imposed on motor vehicles in the city's ZTL (Limited Traffic Zone). Several motorcycle rental companies operate in and around Pisa, providing options for those who prefer to explore the city on two wheels. This mode of transport is ideal for navigating Pisa's streets and enjoying the freedom to park closer to various attractions. Rental details and options can be found by checking with local providers such as [Moto Rent Pisa](http://www.motorentpisa.com) or similar services.

Discovering Pisa by Bicycle

Cycling is becoming an increasingly popular way to explore Pisa, thanks to the city's well-developed cycling infrastructure. Pisa offers dedicated bike lanes and paths, making it a cyclist-friendly destination. Numerous bike rental companies are available, providing both standard bikes and electric options. Renting a bicycle allows you to avoid the traffic restrictions faced by cars and motorbikes.

For bike rental services, visit local providers like [Pisa Bike Rental](http://www.pisabikerental.com) or similar establishments.

Getting Around Pisa on Foot

While Pisa is not the smallest city, its historic center is easily navigable by foot. Walking allows visitors to thoroughly enjoy the city's rich architectural and cultural offerings at a leisurely pace. The compact nature of the historic center makes it practical to explore on foot, offering a more immersive experience of Pisa's charm and attractions. This mode of transportation is ideal for those who want to closely examine the city's landmarks and enjoy its vibrant atmosphere.

Weather and Best Time to Visit

Spring (April to June)

Spring is a delightful time to visit Pisa. The weather is mild and pleasant, with temperatures typically ranging from 15°C to 25°C (59°F to 77°F). This season offers a comfortable climate for exploring the city, and while tourist activity is moderate, it's generally less crowded compared to peak seasons. This is an ideal period for those who prefer to avoid large crowds while enjoying the city's attractions and outdoor spaces.

Summer (July to August)

Summer in Pisa can be quite hot, with temperatures ranging from 25°C to 35°C (77°F to 95°F). This is the peak tourist season, meaning that the city is bustling with visitors, and popular sites such as the Leaning Tower of Pisa may experience long queues. If you don't mind the heat and the crowds, summer offers vibrant city life and numerous events. It's essential to plan ahead and book accommodations and tickets in advance to avoid the peak season's inconveniences.

Autumn (September to October)

Autumn is a wonderful time to visit Pisa. The temperatures are comfortable, ranging from 15°C to 25°C (59°F to 77°F), and the number of tourists decreases compared to summer. This season offers a more relaxed experience, with fewer crowds and more enjoyable weather for sightseeing. It's a great time for leisurely exploration and to experience the city's cultural events and local festivals without the summer rush.

Winter (November to February)

Winter in Pisa is relatively mild, with temperatures ranging from 5°C to 15°C (41°F to 59°F). This is the off-season, which means fewer tourists and a more peaceful experience at the city's attractions. Although the weather can be cool, it's still pleasant enough to enjoy the city's sites and activities without the crowds. This season offers a quieter atmosphere for those who prefer a more serene visit and the opportunity to explore Pisa at a slower pace.

Pisa on a Budget & Travel Tips

When planning your trip to Pisa, you should budget approximately $129 (€120) per day. On average, visitors spend about $54 (€50) on meals, $12 (€11) on local transportation, and $128 (€119) on accommodation. This daily budget encompasses the basic expenses needed to enjoy the city comfortably.

For a one-week stay in Pisa, the typical cost for two people amounts to around $1,804 (€1,678). This figure includes accommodation, meals, local transportation, and sightseeing expenses. For a single traveler, a one-week trip generally costs about $902 (€839).

A two-week stay in Pisa costs approximately $1,804 (€1,678) for one person and $3,608 (€3,355) for two people. This estimate covers similar expenses including accommodation, dining, local transportation, and sightseeing.

If you are planning a longer stay, a one-month visit to Pisa costs around $3,866 (€3,595) for an individual and $7,732 (€7,190) for two people. Extended stays typically reduce the daily cost per person due to shared accommodation and potential savings on longer-term rentals.

Cost Breakdown

- Accommodation: For a double occupancy room, the average cost is $60 (€119) per night.
- Local Transportation: The average daily expenditure is $12 (€11).
- Food: Expect to spend around $54 (€50) per day on meals.
- Entertainment: A daily budget of about $21 (€20) is typical for entertainment and activities.

Note

Prices can fluctuate based on travel style, duration of stay, and other factors. Traveling with a family or in a group may reduce individual costs due to shared expenses and discounted rates for children. Additionally, longer trips may lead to lower daily expenses as you take advantage of extended stay discounts and slower travel rates.

Budget Tips for Visiting Pisa

Pisa's fame largely comes from its iconic Leaning Tower, which can make the city quite expensive, particularly during peak tourist seasons. However, exploring beyond the primary tourist sites can offer a more affordable and less crowded experience.

Here are several strategies to help you save money while visiting Pisa:

Avoid Peak Summer Months

Summer in Pisa is characterized by high temperatures, large crowds, and elevated prices. The influx of tourists increases accommodation costs and makes it harder to find a place to stay. To enjoy pleasant weather and fewer crowds, consider traveling during the shoulder seasons—spring or autumn—when prices are lower and the city is more relaxed.

Purchase a Combination Monument Ticket

If you plan to visit multiple attractions, a combination ticket is a cost-effective option. A comprehensive ticket, which includes access to all major historic sites and the Leaning Tower, is priced at €27. Alternatively, a ticket covering only the main sights, excluding the tower, is available for €10. Single-entry tickets cost €7 each, while a ticket to the tower alone is €20. By opting for the combination ticket, you can save money if you visit at least three attractions.

Utilize Hotel Rewards Points

To reduce accommodation costs, consider signing up for hotel credit cards that offer rewards points. Many credit cards provide sign-up bonuses that include one or two free nights. Use these points to cover your stay and enjoy a cost-free room. Research the basics of hotel rewards programs to maximize your points and make the most of your travel budget.

Skip Unwanted Bread Charges

Some restaurants in Pisa add a charge for bread or breadsticks placed on the table without informing you beforehand. To avoid unnecessary expenses, decline the bread if you do not want it or inform the staff that you do not wish to be served this item.

opt for Affordable Dining Options

Eating out at every meal can quickly add up. To save money, consider purchasing inexpensive meals like paninis and pizza by the slice, which are available for just a few euros. For those on a tight budget, cooking your own meals is a great alternative.

Grocery prices are reasonable, and preparing your own food can significantly reduce your overall expenses.

Use Couchsurfing for Accommodation

Accommodation costs in Pisa can be high. To save money, use Couchsurfing to find free places to stay with local hosts. Not only will this method save you money, but it also provides an opportunity to connect with locals who can offer valuable insights and recommendations.

Join a Free Walking Tour

Participating in a free walking tour is an excellent way to explore Pisa's history and ensure you see important landmarks. These tours typically last a few hours and are a good way to spend part of your day. Remember to tip the tour guide to show your appreciation for their service.

Bring a Reusable Water Bottle

The tap water in Pisa is safe to drink, so carrying a reusable water bottle can help you save money and minimize plastic waste.

CHAPTER 3
PISA TOP ATTRACTIONS

Pisa, once a pivotal Roman port city, has undergone significant transformation over the centuries. Originally situated on the coast, the city is now located approximately 10 kilometers inland due to sedimentation of the Arno River. The city's prominence surged in 1063 when Pisa's navy played a crucial role in the defeat of the Saracens in Messina and Palermo. This victory marked the beginning of Pisa's dominance over Mediterranean trade routes. To commemorate these successes, the city constructed its cathedral, funded by the spoils from its naval expeditions during the First Crusade.

During its peak, Pisa was a hub of commerce and industry, renowned across Europe for its architectural, sculptural, and artistic achievements. The city's naval power, however, suffered a blow in 1284 when the Genoese navy defeated it. Subsequently, in 1406, Pisa came under the control of Florence. Despite this change in governance, the Medici family, who ruled Florence, took a personal interest in Pisa's development. They invested in the construction of bridges and canals, ensuring the city's continued prosperity.

Pisa is also notable for being the birthplace of Galileo Galilei (1564-1642). According to legend, Galileo was inspired to invent the pendulum clock by the swaying chandelier in the cathedral. Today, Pisa's main attractions, including the Leaning Tower, Cathedral, Baptistery, and Campo Santo, are clustered together in the Piazza dei Miracoli (Field of Miracles), which is designated as a UNESCO World Heritage site.

For dining and shopping in Pisa, head to Via Maffi, which connects the Piazza dei Miracoli with the vibrant Borgo Stretto. This area is filled with an array of shops, cafés, and restaurants, offering a taste of local life and cuisine.

Marina di Pisa Beach

Marina di Pisa, situated just a short drive or train ride from the city of Pisa, is an ideal destination for those seeking a seaside escape. This coastal area is accessible in about 10 to 20 minutes from Pisa, whether by car, bus, or train. The northern part of Marina di Pisa features small stretches of sandy and pebbly beaches, while the southern end offers more expansive and finer sandy shores. These beaches are equipped with various tourist facilities and are protected by breakwater rocks, which shield the area from sea storms. The picturesque bays along the coastline provide stunning views and make Marina di Pisa a popular choice for a day trip. You can enjoy local accommodations, dining options, and nightlife if they decide to extend their stay in this charming Tuscan seaside resort.

Tirrenia Beach

Tirrenia is renowned for its superior resort amenities compared to Marina di Pisa. This area boasts a range of luxury hotels and more budget-friendly lodging options, alongside excellent dining establishments and vibrant nightlife. The beach in Tirrenia stands out with its extensive facilities, catering to a variety of water and land sports, including sailing, underwater fishing, horseback riding, golf, and beach volleyball. Tirrenia's well-developed infrastructure connects it seamlessly to major Tuscan roads, making it easily accessible from across the Italian peninsula, particularly from Pisa. The beaches in Tirrenia are a major attraction, drawing tourists from Pisa and other nearby Tuscan locales for their pristine conditions and comprehensive recreational offerings.

Marina di Vecchiano Beach

Marina di Vecchiano boasts a pristine, 4-kilometer-long sandy beach framed by golden dunes and lush pine woods, nestled within the Migliarino San Rossore Massaciuccoli Nature Park.

This beach offers an unparalleled natural setting, providing a serene escape from the more crowded tourist spots in Tuscany. Its tranquil environment is complemented by modern amenities that blend seamlessly into the natural surroundings, catering to both sunbathers and those seeking more active pursuits. Marina di Vecchiano is an excellent choice for a day trip from Pisa, offering a refreshing alternative to more bustling destinations. Visitors can enjoy the unspoiled beauty and the range of activities available, including sunbathing and exploration of the surrounding natural park.

Calambrone Beach

Calambrone features an expansive sandy shoreline bordered by the vast Tombolo forest, which is part of the San Rossore Nature Park. This beach is currently experiencing significant development to enhance its tourist infrastructure. Despite these changes, Calambrone Beach remains a popular destination due to its well-maintained facilities and ideal conditions for water sports such as sailing and windsurfing. The clear waters and spacious sand area continue to attract visitors looking for a blend of relaxation and active recreation, making it a valuable option for those exploring Tuscany's coastal attractions.

The Leaning Tower of Pisa

The Leaning Tower of Pisa, or La Torre Pendente, is an iconic structure that draws visitors from around the globe. Construction began in 1173 during Pisa's zenith as a maritime power, with the tower's design reflecting the cathedral's façade. Early in its construction, the tower began to lean due to unstable foundation soil.

Despite attempts to correct the tilt by adjusting the construction and adding counterweights, work was halted in the late 12th century. In the 14th century, the upper levels were angled to mitigate the lean. The bell chamber was added between 1350 and 1372 by Tommaso Pisano.

The tower was closed in 1990 for significant restoration due to increasing tilt and risk of collapse. It reopened in 2001 with the tilt reduced from 5.5 to approximately 3.99 degrees, with the top misaligned by 3.9 meters. The structure's curve reflects the various attempts to correct its tilt throughout its history. For more details, visit the official site at [Opera della Primaziale Pisana](http://www.opapisa.it/en). The tower is located at Piazza dei Miracoli, Pisa.

Cathedral of Santa Maria Assunta

The Cathedral of Santa Maria Assunta, a prime example of Pisan Romanesque architecture, is distinguished by its white marble façade and expansive five-aisled basilica layout. Designed by architect Buscheto, construction began in 1063 following Pisa's victory over the Saracens, and the cathedral was consecrated in 1118, despite being incomplete.

The façade is adorned with intricate arcading, and the interior features a grand oval dome. Notable is the 13th- to 14th-century mosaic of Christ with the Virgin and John the Evangelist by Cimabue, and the bronze Porta di San Ranieri doors, which depict scenes from the lives of Christ and the Virgin.

The cathedral's highlight is Giovanni Pisano's pulpit, crafted between 1302 and 1311. This pulpit, with its rounded forms and dynamic style, contrasts with the more angular pulpit by his father Nicola in the nearby baptistery. Giovanni Pisano's pulpit is supported by columns and adorned with figures of Archangel Michael, Hercules, and Christ, surrounded by reliefs of New

Testament scenes. The cathedral is located at Piazza dei Miracoli, Pisa. Visit http://www.opapisa.it/ for more information.

Baptistery

Located west of the Cathedral of Pisa, the Baptistery, initiated in 1153, mirrors the cathedral's design with its use of similar materials and architectural motifs. Over its two-century construction period, the Baptistery evolved from Romanesque to Gothic styles. Nicola Pisano began work on the project in 1260, followed by his son Giovanni Pisano between 1285 and

1293. The Baptistery features a conical dome supported by four pillars and eight columns, creating an impressive visual effect of light and solemnity.

The main highlight is the marble pulpit by Nicola Pisano, crafted in 1260. This pulpit, renowned for its detailed relief panels depicting New Testament scenes, stands as a masterwork of Romanesque sculpture. The Baptistery also houses Guido da Como's font from 1246 and various figures created by students of Nicola and Giovanni Pisano. The acoustics of the Baptistery are particularly noteworthy and are often demonstrated by guides. For more information, visit the Baptistery at Piazza dei Miracoli, Pisa, website: https://www.opapisa.it/visita/battistero/.

Campo Santo (Sacred Field)

Legend has it that Archbishop Ubaldo dei Lanfranchi returned from the Fourth Crusade with sacred soil from Golgotha for the citizens of Pisa to be buried in. The construction of the Camposanto, or Sacred Field, began in 1278. This large rectangular cloister features Gothic-tracery arches that open into the courtyard. The cloister's floor is adorned with the graves of Pisan patricians and Roman sarcophagi along the walls. Originally covered in 14th- and 15th-century frescoes, the

Camposanto suffered significant damage in 1944 when a fire caused by artillery bombardment melted the lead roof, destroying or severely damaging many frescoes.

However, the fire revealed original artist sketches called sinópie on the walls. These sketches are now displayed at the Museo delle Sinópie, along with reproductions of the lost frescoes. The remaining frescoes have been painstakingly restored and returned to the cloister. Visit the Camposanto at Piazza dei Miracoli, Pisa.

Museo dell'Opera del Duomo (Cathedral Museum)

Situated on the Campo dei Miracoli, the Museo dell'Opera del Duomo is a well-curated museum offering insight into the art and craftsmanship of Pisa's cathedral complex. Despite being one of the less-visited sites, the museum provides a valuable understanding of the period's art, alongside an excellent view of the Leaning Tower from its second-floor windows.

The museum houses an extensive collection of treasures, including silversmith works, embroideries, tombs, sculptures, and paintings. Many of these pieces, originally part of the cathedral's exterior, have been moved indoors for preservation.

Noteworthy items include the bronze griffin, Borgognone's wooden crucifix, the Citharoedus David, Limoges caskets, and works by Giovanni Pisano, including his Madonnas, a small ivory statue, and the Crocifisso d'Elci. The museum also features a Roman bust of Julius Caesar, familiar from history books. For further details, visit the Museo dell'Opera del Duomo at Piazza dei Miracoli, Pisa, website: https://www.opapisa.it/visita/museo-dellopera/

Murale Tuttomondo by Keith Haring

In 1989, American artist Keith Haring, after meeting a student from Pisa, was commissioned to create a mural on the rear wall of Sant'Antonio Abate Church. This work, known as Tuttomondo (meaning "all the world"), spans 180 square meters, making it one of Europe's largest murals. Haring completed the mural in one week. Tuttomondo is one of the few outdoor pieces Haring created for permanent public display and was one of his final works before his death in 1990. The mural features 30 figures, including humans, animals like dolphins and bats, all rendered in Haring's distinctive cartoon style. The vibrant colors and dynamic composition embody Haring's message of harmony among people, animals, and nature. For more information, you can visit the mural at P.za V. Emanuele II, 18, 56125 Pisa PI, Italy

Arsenals & Museum of Ancient Ships

Constructed between 1548 and 1588 under Grand Duke Cosimo I de' Medici, the Arsenals were designed to enhance Pisa's naval strength and revive the city's maritime prominence. These extensive arcaded sheds were used to build 50-meter-long galleys and were situated within the Cittadella, which dates back to 1160. The only remaining structure from the Cittadella is the San'Agnese tower. The Guelfa Tower, erected in the early 1400s, offers panoramic views of Pisa and the Arno River and was rebuilt after World War II damage.

Following 1543, the Cittadella served as artillery barracks and later as stables for the Dragon knights. The Arsenals now house the Museum of Ancient Ships, which showcases artifacts from a

1998 excavation that uncovered over 30 ancient ships from between the 2nd century BC and the 5th century AD.

These ships, representing various eras from the Etruscans to the Roman Empire's decline, are displayed alongside recovered artifacts that illustrate ancient maritime life. The museum is located at Lungarno Ranieri Simonelli 16, Pisa. For more details, visit [Museum of Ancient Ships](https://www.navidipisa.it/en/).

Santa Maria della Spina

The Church of Santa Maria della Spina, situated on the left bank of the Arno River, is renowned for its Gothic beauty. Originally a modest oratory directly on the river, the church faced severe foundation issues and was dismantled and relocated in 1871. The church is named after a thorn from Christ's crown of thorns, which was brought from the Holy Land. Its richly decorated Gothic façade features two doorways and three distinctive gables, each adorned with small rose windows. On the south side, a series of arches encloses doorways and windows, while higher up, a niche displays figures of Christ and the Apostles. The church's tabernacles, originally housing statues, now have replicas with the originals displayed at the Museo Nazionale. The Madonna del Latte statue inside the church is a replica; the original is also at the museum. The church is located at Lungarno Gambacorti, Pisa. For more information, contact +39 050 550100

Borgo Stretto

Borgo Stretto, located between the Pisa train station and Piazza dei Miracoli, is a picturesque, narrow street dating back to the 14th and 15th centuries. The street is flanked by charming medieval buildings and covered arcades, providing shelter from the elements. It features a blend of boutique shops, brand-name stores, cafés, and street vendors, making it a lively destination for both shopping and strolling. A notable landmark on this street is Casa Bocca, situated at the corner of Borgo Stretto and Via Mercanti, which is the birthplace of Galileo Galilei. The area is consistently bustling with locals and visitors alike.

Palazzo dei Cavalieri

The Palazzo dei Cavalieri, also known as the Palazzo della Carovana, is situated in Piazza dei Cavalieri (Knights' Square).

Originally the Palazzo degli Anziani (Palace of the Elders), it was transformed into its current grandiose form starting in 1562 by architect Giorgio Vasari. The building, named for its role in training knights of the Order of St. Stephen, features an elaborate façade adorned with sgraffito decorations, coats of arms, and busts of six Medici Grand Dukes, ranging from Cosimo I to Cosimo III. The striking double staircase and the projecting roof enhance its stately appearance. Since 1810, the palazzo has been home to the Scuola Normale Superiore, a prestigious institution founded by Napoleon. In front of the palazzo stands a statue of Cosimo I sculpted by Piero Francavilla. On the north side of the piazza, you'll find the Palazzo dell'Orologio, constructed in 1607 for the Order of St. Stephen and incorporating remnants of medieval towers. The Palazzo dei Cavalieri is located at Piazza dei Cavalieri, Pisa.

Palazzo Blu

Palazzo Blu, officially known as Palazzo Giuli Rosselmini Gualandi, is renowned for its extensive collection of Italian art spanning from the 16th to the 20th centuries. In addition to paintings, the palace houses fine furniture and early coins. It also hosts temporary exhibitions covering a range of topics, including science, cinema, and individual artists such as M.C. Escher and Amedeo Modigliani. Palazzo Blu is located at Lungarno Gambacorti 9, Pisa.

Basilica Romanica di San Piero a Grado

Situated on the route to Pisa's marina, the Basilica Romanica di San Piero a Grado is a 10th-century church constructed on the site where tradition holds that St. Peter arrived in Italy in 44 AD. Historically, this area was once part of the Mediterranean Sea, though the coast has since receded.

The basilica, which underwent construction and alterations over 200 years, features a vibrant collection of frescoes within its interior. Excavations at the back of the church have uncovered the foundations of an earlier Paleo-Christian church and even older Roman structures. The basilica is located at Via Livornese, Pisa. Visit http://www.sanpieroagrado.it/ for more information.

Orto Botanico (Botanic Garden)

The Orto Botanico, also known as the Orto Botanico dell'Università di Pisa, is Europe's oldest university botanical garden, established by Cosimo I de' Medici in the 1550s. Visitors can explore a variety of botanical environments, including herb gardens, a collection of rare trees, water features, and historic greenhouses, one of which is Europe's earliest iron-framed glasshouse. The garden also includes a late 1500s botany school with a distinctive seashell-decorated façade. This garden provides a tranquil escape amidst Pisa's rich array of Renaissance art. It is located at Via Luca Ghini 5, Pisa.

Santo Stefano dei Cavalieri

Santo Stefano dei Cavalieri, situated in Piazza dei Cavalieri, was originally constructed between 1565 and 1569 and later adorned with a marble façade designed by Giovanni de' Medici between 1594 and 1606. The church's 17th-century side wings, originally changing rooms for the knights of the Order of St. Stephen, were later incorporated as aisles.

The church, designed by Giorgio Vasari, creates a unique impression with its aisleless nave. Inside, the coffered ceiling panels depict the history of the Order, and the walls display trophies and captured enemy flags from Pisa's conflicts. The high altar, dating from 1709, is elaborately decorated and features a Baroque organ and a throne representing Pope Stephen I. The church is located in Piazza dei Cavalieri, Pisa.

Piazza delle Gondole

The Piazza delle Gondole, located adjacent to one of Pisa's medieval gates, is a small square featuring a basin where boats once docked. This historic site reflects Pisa's maritime past and offers a glimpse into the city's earlier connections to water transport.

Museo Nazionale di San Matteo (National Museum of San Matteo)

Located in the former Benedictine Convent of San Matteo, the Museo Nazionale di San Matteo offers a deep dive into Tuscan art spanning from the 12th to the 15th centuries. The museum houses a significant collection of sculptures and paintings from the Pisan schools. Among the highlights are original statues by Giovanni Pisano, including those from the Baptistery and the Madonna del Latte (c. 1340) from the Church of Santa Maria della Spina. The museum also showcases exquisite examples of illuminated manuscripts and religious paintings by 12th- and 13th-century artists. The museum is situated at Lungarno Mediceo, Piazza San Matteo 1, Pisa. For more information, visit https://museitoscana.cultura.gov.it/

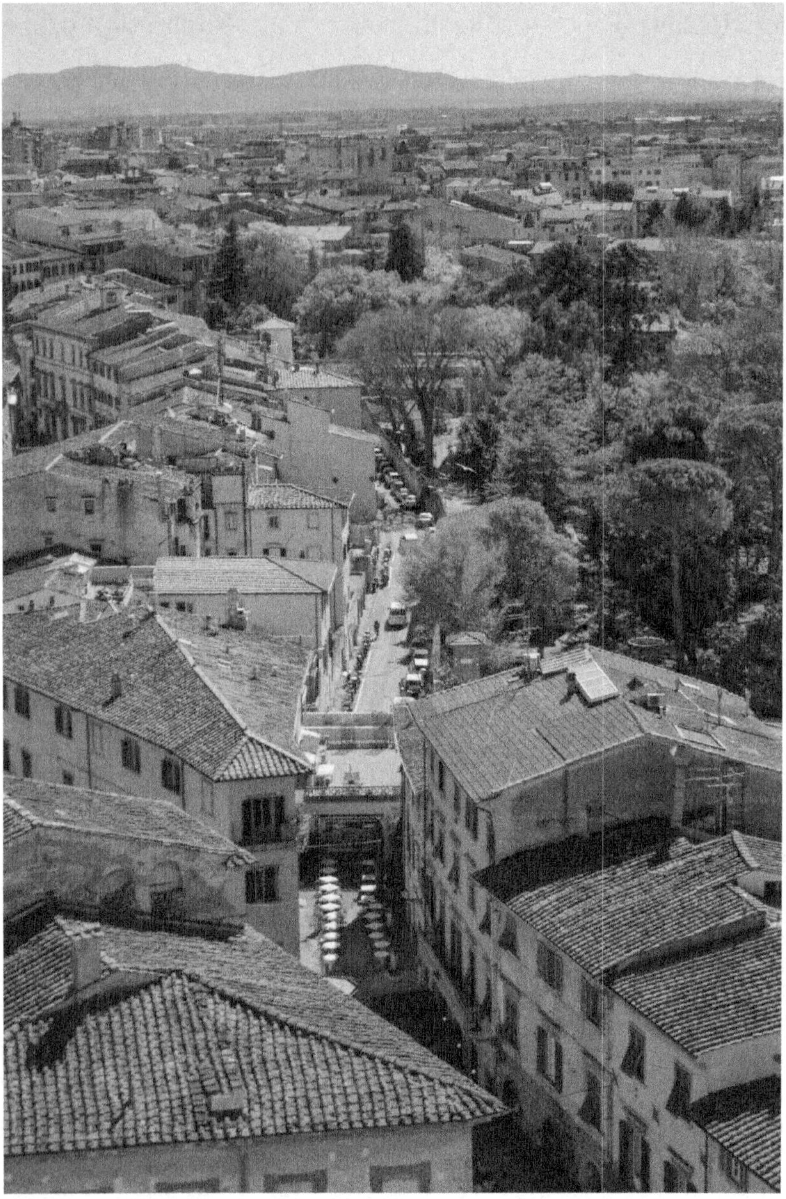

CHAPTER 4
5-DAY ITINERARIES IN PISA

Day 1 | Morning

Leaning Tower of Pisa

The Leaning Tower of Pisa, a renowned architectural marvel, stands as an independent bell tower of the Pisa Cathedral, situated in Piazza del Duomo. This 54.5-meter-high tower, built between 1173 and 1350, is famous for its unintended tilt caused by unstable foundation soil. Originally constructed with six trophies from Pisa's fleet, the tower features white marble and 213 arches per floor. Visitors can climb the 294 spiral steps for panoramic views of Pisa. To manage the lean, a stabilization project in 1998 involved attaching cables and removing soil. Tickets cost 18 EUR, and it's advisable to book in advance through the official website to avoid long lines. Access to the summit is limited to 15 people per group, with each visit capped at 30 minutes. For a detailed history introduction and guided ascent, arrive early at the designated meeting spot. Alternatively, visitors can explore the Piazza del Duomo and nearby pedestrian streets, where local crafts are sold. Location: Piazza del Duomo, 56126 Pisa PI, Italy

Day 1 | Afternoon

Piazza del Duomo

After exploring the Leaning Tower of Pisa, take the opportunity to visit the Piazza del Duomo, also known as the Miracle Square. This historic square is open from 7:00 AM to midnight and is renowned for its stunning architectural ensemble, including the Pisa Cathedral, the Baptistery, the Leaning Tower, and the Camposanto Monumentale (cemetery).

Designated a UNESCO World Heritage Site in 1987, the square represents a pinnacle of medieval art and architecture.

The Pisa Cathedral, at the heart of the square, was constructed in the 12th century and exemplifies medieval Romanesque architecture with its distinctive "Pisa Romanesque" style, incorporating Byzantine mosaic elements. Adjacent to the cathedral is the Baptistery, which combines Romanesque and Gothic influences. Its interior, accessible via a spiral staircase, features a double dome and white marble, enhancing its aesthetic appeal.

The Leaning Tower of Pisa, a bell tower for the cathedral, is famous for its unintended tilt. Initially, the tower tilted about 1 millimeter per year during construction, leading to periodic halts and ongoing stabilization efforts. The adjacent Camposanto Monumentale is a notable cemetery with impressive tombstones, sculptures, and frescoes in its cloisters.

The expansive lawn within the square offers a pleasant resting area where visitors can take photos, purchase souvenirs, and enjoy snacks. Location: Piazza del Duomo, 56126 Pisa PI, Italy

Day 1 | Evening

Bagni di Pisa Palace & Thermal Spa

For a relaxing end to your day, consider visiting Bagni di Pisa Palace & Thermal Spa, situated in the scenic San Giuliano Terme area. This luxurious spa offers a range of amenities designed to enhance your comfort and rejuvenation. Facilities include accessibility features for disabled guests, Wi-Fi, parking, room service, and airport transfer. Rooms are equipped with modern conveniences such as LCD/plasma TVs, non-smoking options, air conditioning, heating, and work desks.

The hotel features a tranquil atmosphere complemented by its recreational facilities, which include a hot tub, fitness center, sauna, and hot spring bath. Additionally, there's a golf course located within 3 kilometers for those interested in a round of golf. Whether you're looking to unwind or simply enjoy a serene environment, Bagni di Pisa Palace & Thermal Spa provides an ideal retreat. Location: San Giuliano Terme, Pisa, Italy

Day 2 | Morning

Battistero (Baptistery)

The Battistero, located in Piazza del Duomo, Pisa, is an architectural gem combining Romanesque and Gothic styles. Its prominent 35-meter-wide dome and elaborately carved doors create a striking exterior. Inside, the building is renowned for its excellent lighting and acoustic effects, making it a captivating place to explore.

The Battistero is open daily from 10:00 AM to 5:00 PM, and admission is free. Allocate approximately 1 to 2 hours to fully appreciate this unique structure. Address: Piazza del Duomo, 23, 56126 Pisa PI, Italy

Day 2 | Afternoon

Cattedrale di Santa Maria Assunta (Cathedral of Santa Maria Assunta)

Following your visit to the Battistero, head to the Cattedrale di Santa Maria Assunta, also known as the Cathedral of the Assumption of Our Lady. Situated in the same Miracle Square, this cathedral is celebrated for its distinctive architectural style and serene ambiance. It is open from 1:00 PM to 8:00 PM on Sundays and from 10:00 AM to 8:00 PM on other days. Entry is free. Plan to spend 1 to 2 hours here to fully take in its beauty. Address: Piazza del Duomo, Pisa, Italy

Day 2 | Evening

Pisa Tower Plaza

For a comfortable place to stay after your explorations, consider the Pisa Tower Plaza. This modern hotel offers a range of amenities and is conveniently located near the Natural Park of San Rossore, just 200 meters from Pisa San Rossore train station and a 10-minute walk from the city's main attractions. Rooms and suites provide stunning views of Piazza dei Miracoli and the iconic Leaning Tower of Pisa. Location: Near the Natural Park of San Rossore, Pisa, Italy

Day 3 | Morning

Piazza dei Cavalieri

Piazza dei Cavalieri is a historic square centrally located in Pisa. Despite its modest size, the square is surrounded by significant academic and architectural landmarks, such as the esteemed

Scuola Normale Superiore and the University of Pisa's Faculty of Law and Faculty of Letters. This area, marked by its scholarly atmosphere, provides a pleasant environment for visitors to explore. The square is accessible around the clock and admission is free. Allocate about 1 to 2 hours to soak in the surroundings. Address: Piazza dei Cavalieri, 56100 Pisa PI, Italy

Day 3 | Afternoon

Camposanto Monumentale

After visiting Piazza dei Cavalieri, head to Camposanto Monumentale, a historic cemetery known for its striking architecture. The Camposanto, enclosed by a white marble wall and a cloistered courtyard, is the final resting place of many notable figures from Pisa. It features over 600 tombstones and sarcophagi adorned with intricate reliefs, while the cloisters are embellished with detailed frescoes.

The cemetery is open 24 hours a day and entry is free. Plan to spend around 1 hour here. Address: Piazza del Duomo, 17, 56126 Pisa PI, Italy

Day 3 | Evening

Rinascimento Bed & Breakfast

For a convenient and comfortable stay in Pisa, Rinascimento Bed & Breakfast is an excellent choice. This accommodation provides simply furnished rooms equipped with air conditioning, a TV, and a private bathroom. Located just 700 meters from the Leaning Tower and Pisa Cathedral, it offers easy access to the city's main attractions. The rooms feature Tuscan-style decor and painted ceilings, with some including a kitchenette. The property is 1 km from Pisa Centrale Train Station and about a 10-minute drive from Pisa Galilei Airport. Address: Residence Gorkij, Central Pisa, Italy

Day 4 | Morning

Church of Santa Maria della Spina

Start your day at the Church of Santa Maria della Spina, a small yet striking Gothic church situated along the Arno River, adjacent to the Middle Bridge. The church's intricate Gothic architecture offers a refreshing contrast to the grand cathedrals typically found in Pisa. Spend 1 to 2 hours exploring this unique chapel, which stands out for its ornate detailing and historical charm. Address: Lungarno Gambacorti, 56125 Pisa PI, Italy

Day 4 | Afternoon

Palazzo della Sapienza

Next, visit Palazzo della Sapienza, an essential stop before concluding your exploration of Pisa. This building, which serves as the library for the University of Pisa, is a landmark of local architectural significance.

The building's aesthetic is a fine example of local design, making it a worthwhile visit. Allocate 1 to 2 hours for this stop. Admission is free. Address: Via Curtatone e Montanara, Pisa PI, Italy

Day 4 | Evening

Borgo Pignano

For a relaxing evening, head to Borgo Pignano, a picturesque retreat nestled amidst the hills of Volterra and surrounded by 300 hectares of private gardens and woods. The property features an outdoor pool, a children's club, and a restaurant specializing in regional cuisine. The accommodations, which include rooms, suites, and apartments, are decorated with 19th-century artwork and frescoes. Most rooms offer a seating area, and some include a balcony or furnished patio. Borgo Pignano emphasizes sustainability with an eco-friendly heating system and produces its own olive oil and fruit.

The property is located 15 km from Volterra and a 20-minute drive from San Gimignano. On-site parking is available. Address: Borgo Pignano, Volterra, Italy

Day 5 | Morning

Keith Haring Mural

Begin your day by visiting the Keith Haring mural located on Piazza Vittorio Emanuele II in Pisa. This vibrant fresco, painted by the renowned artist Keith Haring, can be spotted on the wall behind the Monastery of St. Anthony. The mural, which carries a powerful message of world peace, is situated conveniently along the route from the train station to the Leaning Tower of Pisa. Address: Piazza Vittorio Emanuele II, 56125 Pisa, Italy

Day 5 | Afternoon

La Fortezza di Volterra

In the afternoon, make your way to La Fortezza di Volterra, an essential stop to experience the historical essence of the region. This fortress is a testament to the city of Volterra's rich history, dating back to the 5th century BC. The fortress, still retaining its medieval charm, stands as a significant symbol of Volterra's past political and economic importance. The town is also known for its alabaster production, with small alabaster sculptures available in local shops. While not a major tourist hub, Volterra gained international attention as a filming location for "Twilight Saga - New Moon." Allocate 1 to 2 hours for your visit. Admission is free, and the fortress is accessible around the clock. Address: Rampa di Castello, 4, 56048 Volterra PI, Italy

CHAPTER 5
RESTAURANT RECOMMENDATION

Pizzeria Quarto D'ora Italiano

Located at Via Santa Maria, 117, just minutes from Piazza dei Miracoli, Pizzeria Quarto D'ora Italiano offers authentic wood-fired Neapolitan pizza with thick edges and thin centers. It's a cozy spot known for quality and reasonable prices, with standout dishes like tagliata di manzo (beef steak). Contact them for more details at +39 059 991 1380.

Trattoria Sant'Omobono

Situated at Piazza S. Omobono, 6, Trattoria Sant'Omobono delivers simplicity and authenticity with homemade local dishes such as trippa alla pisana and baccalà. Known for its relaxed atmosphere and affordability, it's a great spot for genuine Pisa cuisine.

Osteria di Culegna

At Via Mercanti 25, Osteria di Culegna features a rustic, friendly ambiance with dishes like peposo (beef stew) and ravioli with

Chianina beef ragù. Open Mon-Sat from 12:30pm-3pm and 7:45pm-11pm, reservations are recommended. For details, call +39 050 57 64 26.

050

The contemporary 050, located at Via delle Piagge 15, boasts a warm interior with a diverse menu featuring fresh vegetables and gluten-free options. Owner Marco sources organic ingredients for dishes like beetroot risotto and pasta with calamari. For reservations, contact +39 050 54 31 06 or visit biosteria050.it.

Alle Bandierine

Located at Via San Francesco, 21, Alle Bandierine serves classic Tuscan pasta and regional dishes like octopus and four-cheese sauce. The restaurant, with its charming décor, offers a selection of local wines and desserts like apple cake with vanilla ice cream. For reservations, call +39 050 50 00 00 or visit ristorantealleandierine.it. Prices are moderate.

Pizzeria Il Montino

At Vicolo del Monte 1, Pizzeria Il Montino is renowned for its cecina (chickpea flatbread) and traditional pizzas such as Pizza

Pisana. Open Tuesday-Saturday from 10:30am-3pm and 5:30pm-10:30pm, it's a popular spot for locals. For details, call +39 050 59 86 95. Prices are budget-friendly.

La Pergoletta

Located at Via della Storia, 6, La Pergoletta offers inventive seasonal dishes like green gnocchi with blue cheese and seafood. Known for its fresh, relaxed ambiance under a live vine canopy, the restaurant is open daily. For reservations, call +39 050 54 24 58 or visit ristorantelapergoletta.com. Prices are moderate to high.

Gusto al 129 Pizzeria

Gusto al 129 in the San Francesco neighborhood serves high-quality, long-fermented pizzas with fresh ingredients. Popular for its varied menu including classic and unique pizzas like sapor'e mar, it's known for excellent service. Check out their sweet pizzas with Nutella. For more information, visit their website or contact them directly. Prices are moderate.

Branzo

At Via della Marina, 10, Branzo is a seafood restaurant offering creative dishes like grilled octopus with Jerusalem artichoke mash. Known for its international flair and fresh, local ingredients, it's a top spot for seafood lovers.

Trattoria da Stelio

Trattoria da Stelio, at P.za Dante Alighieri, 11, offers a traditional, cozy dining experience with daily-changing menus of pasta, meats, and seafood since 1965. Expect affordable, homemade Tuscan dishes in a lively atmosphere with outdoor seating on warm days. Reservations are not necessary; be prepared for potential wait times.

Numero 11

Numero 11, or Numeroundici, at Via S. Martino, 47, is a casual spot with long tables for communal dining. This self-service restaurant provides large portions of traditional Tuscan food, with a focus on creating a homely atmosphere where you order at the counter and clear your own table. Website: http://www.numeroundici.it/

Hostaria Le Repubbliche Marinare Pisa

At Hostaria Le Repubbliche Marinare Pisa, located at Vicolo Ricciardi, 8, enjoy high-end seafood dishes with elegant decor and large portions, costing around $40 per person plus drinks.

The menu features items like fish soup and fresh seafood pasta, with a complimentary digestif enhancing the experience. Website: https://www.repubblichemarinare.eu/

La Grotta

La Grotta, at Via San Francesco, 103, offers a romantic, cave-like setting with Etruscan dishes. Popular options include Buffalo Mozzarella Ravioli and traditional Panna Cotta for dessert.

The cozy atmosphere makes it a local favorite for intimate dining. Website: http://www.osterialagrotta.com/

Trattoria Pizzeria Il Montino

Trattoria Pizzeria Il Montino, at Vicolo del Monte, 1, specializes in wood-fired pizzas and quick service, ideal for busy days. Also available are lasagna and roast beef, but the main draw is their pizza, made fresh in view. Website: https://www.pizzeriailmontino.it/

Il Campano

Il Campano, situated at Via Domenico Cavalca, 19, is a renowned Pisan restaurant known for its traditional Tuscan dishes with a modern twist, such as Pappa al Pomodoro and Gnudi. It offers a broad selection of 400 wines, reflecting its rich culinary heritage. Website: https://www.ilcampano.com/

Pane e Vino

At Pane e Vino, Piazza Chiara Gambacorti, 7, enjoy charcuterie boards with fresh mozzarella and Italian cold cuts, paired with a regional wine list. The cozy wine bar has mostly outdoor seating, offering views of the plaza, and also serves Tuscan dishes like Pappa al Pomodoro and Tordello Lucchese. Website: https://facebook.com/EnotecaPaneEVino/

La Pergoletta

La Pergoletta, located at Via delle Belle Torri, 40, features a unique dining room with foliage and a relaxed atmosphere. The mid-tier restaurant offers regional wines and a varied menu including pasta, fish, and steak, with vegetarian options like Courgette Parmigiana and Homemade Ravioli. Website: http://www.ristorantelapergoletta.com/

CHAPTER 6
HOTELS RECOMMENDATION

Palazzo Feroci - Residenza d'epoca

Palazzo Feroci, 500 meters from the Leaning Tower of Pisa, offers air-conditioned apartments with free WiFi, a minibar, and a private bathroom. Guests can enjoy continental or Italian breakfast, bike rentals, and city tours. The property also features a coffee shop and bar. For more details, visit palazzoferoci.it.

The Rif - Boutique Hotel

The Rif - Boutique Hotel, 500 meters from Piazza dei Miracoli, provides air-conditioned rooms, free WiFi, and a hot tub. It has a garden, restaurant with Italian cuisine, and bike rentals. Rooms feature a minibar, flat-screen TV, and some have balconies. Visit [therif.com] for bookings and details.

Palazzo Cini Luxury Rooms

Palazzo Cini, 1.3 km from Leaning Tower of Pisa, offers air-conditioned rooms with flat-screen TVs and private bathrooms. The property provides Italian breakfast delivered to your room.

It is located 2 km from Pisa International Airport. For more information, visit palazzocini.com.

Pisa Tower Plaza

Pisa Tower Plaza, a 15-minute walk from Piazza dei Miracoli, features air-conditioned rooms with free WiFi and a pool with hydromassage jets. The hotel serves a buffet breakfast and Tuscan cuisine. It is a 10-minute drive from Pisa Galileo Airport. For reservations, visit pisatowerplaza.com.

Hotel Di Stefano

Hotel Di Stefano, 5 minutes from the Leaning Tower of Pisa, offers free WiFi, a buffet breakfast, and a rooftop terrace with city views. Rooms feature flat-screen TVs, and the hotel has a 24-hour reception, bar, and tour arrangements. Pisa International Airport is a 10-minute drive away. For more details, visit [hoteldistefano.com].

Residenza d'Epoca Relais I Miracoli

Residenza d'Epoca Relais I Miracoli, 50 meters from the Leaning Tower and Cathedral, features free Wi-Fi, a garden, and rooms with satellite TV. A sweet breakfast with homemade pastries is served daily. The property offers special rates at a nearby garage. Visit [relaisimiracoli.com] for more information.

Rinascimento Bed & Breakfast

Rinascimento Bed & Breakfast, 700 meters from the Leaning Tower, offers air-conditioned rooms with TVs and private bathrooms. Some rooms include kitchenettes. It is 1 km from Pisa Centrale Train Station and a 10-minute drive from the airport. For more details, visit [rinascimento.com].

Hotel Bologna

Hotel Bologna, 5 minutes from the train station, provides free WiFi, a varied buffet breakfast, and a bar with Tuscan tastings. Rooms include minibars and flat-screen TVs, with a 12-minute walk to the Leaning Tower. It offers a shuttle to the airport. Visit [hotelbologna.com] for reservations.

B&B Di Camilla

B&B Di Camilla, 1.2 km from the Leaning Tower of Pisa, offers air-conditioned rooms with free WiFi, a garden, and optional private parking.

Rooms feature flat-screen TVs, private bathrooms, and some include terraces. A coffee shop and bicycle rentals are available.

The nearest airport is Pisa International, 4 km away, with a paid shuttle service. Visit https://www.hotel-bb.com/it/hotel/ for bookings.

Grand Hotel Duomo

Grand Hotel Duomo, 2 minutes from Duomo Square, features air-conditioned rooms with free WiFi, a panoramic roof terrace, and an American bar. The on-site restaurant serves Italian cuisine, and a buffet breakfast is included. The hotel is 4 km from Galileo Galilei Airport. For more information, https://www.grandhotelduomopisa.it/

La Lu Cozy Rooms 2 - Self Check-In

La Lu Cozy Rooms 2, 800 meters from Piazza dei Miracoli, provides air-conditioned rooms with free WiFi, flat-screen TVs, and private bathrooms.

Some rooms have balconies or garden views. A snack bar is on-site, and Pisa International Airport is 4 km away, with a paid shuttle service. For more information, visit https://www.lalucozyrooms.com/lalu/

Il Giardino Dei Semplici

Il Giardino Dei Semplici, under a 5-minute walk from Piazza dei Miracoli, offers air-conditioned rooms with free WiFi, flat-screen TVs, and private bathrooms. Guests can use the shared lounge. Pisa International Airport is 4 km away. For bookings, https://www.ilgiardinodeisemplicipisa.it/

NH Pisa

NH Pisa, opposite Pisa Train Station, offers free Wi-Fi, air-conditioned rooms with satellite TV, and a full American buffet breakfast. The Leaning Tower is a 20-minute walk away, and airport shuttles stop in front of the hotel. For more information, https://www.nh-hotels.com/

Royal Victoria Hotel

Royal Victoria Hotel, overlooking the River Arno, offers elegant rooms and a buffet breakfast. Located in Pisa's historic center, it's close to the Leaning Tower and various dining options. The hotel has been family-managed since 1837, with a private garage and is 2 km from Pisa International Airport. For bookings, https://www.royalvictoria.it/

Palazzo Cini Luxury Rooms in Pisa

Palazzo Cini blends modern amenities with classic charm in a renovated Art Nouveau villa, featuring rooms with jacuzzi bathtubs and beamed ceilings. The property includes a garden with fragrant trees, and breakfast options are available in-room. For bookings, visit https://palazzocinilux.com/.

Rinascimento Bed & Breakfast

Rinascimento Bed & Breakfast offers rooms with frescoed ceilings and Tuscan views, plus terracotta tiles and four-poster beds. Enjoy a breakfast of pastries and cappuccinos in a charming setting with exceptional service. For bookings, visit https://rinascimentopisa.it/

Five Roses Bed & Breakfast

Located a five-minute walk from Pisa train station, Five Roses Bed & Breakfast features three rooms, with options for organic breakfasts and wine-soaked dinners. The Yellow Rose room includes a bunk bed and kitchenette, ideal for families. For bookings, visit, http://www.fiveroses.it/

CHAPTER 7
NIGHTLIFE AND SHOPPING

Nightlife in Pisa

Argini e Margini Pisa

Argini e Margini, located at Scalo dei Renaioli, Lungarno G. Galilei, 56125, +39 342 705 8237, offers a riverside bar and raft with a mix of live music and stylish ambiance from June to September. Check the music before entering on their website: [www.arginiemargini.com]

Arno Vivo

Arno Vivo, situated at Lungarno Buozzi, 56125, +39 331 279 1271, is a popular open-air venue along the Arno River featuring live music and DJ sets from June to September. The music can be heard from a distance; check it out before entering.

Orzo Bruno

Orzo Bruno, located at Via delle Case Dipinte 6-8, Pisa, +39 392 306 0433, offers a relaxed atmosphere with a variety of local craft beers, wines, antipasti, and panini. Visit their website for more info: www.orzobruno.it.

Baribaldi

Baribaldi, found at Piazza Giuseppe Garibaldi 8, Pisa, +39 380 41 37 086, serves cocktails, Tuscan wines, and more in a prime city square. Enjoy the vibrant atmosphere in one of Pisa's main squares.

Vicolo Divino

Vicolo Divino, at Via Filippo Serafini 10, Pisa, +39 377 94 28 446, is a quaint wine bar offering a wide selection of wines and snacks, open Mon-Sat 11:30am-3pm and 6pm-10pm; closed Sun. For more details, email info@vicolodivino.it.

Chupiteria Pisa

Chupiteria Pisa, located at Lungarno Mediceo 59, Pisa, +39 345 24 27 606, serves a vast array of shots daily from 9pm until late. Create your own shot or choose from their extensive menu.

Sunset Café

Sunset Café, at Via Litoranea 40, Marina di Pisa, +39 328 464 0409, offers a romantic beachside setting with excellent long drinks and sunset views, open during spring and summer.

Tree

Tree, situated at Via San Francesco 90, Pisa, +39 333 423 7835, is a rock bar known for its great coffee and cocktails, providing a cozy atmosphere both indoors and outdoors.

La Borsa

La Borsa, located at Piazza Vittorio Emanuele II 1, Pisa, +39 050 50 06 97, is a popular student hangout offering vibrant aperitivos and buffet food. For inquiries, email contact@laborsa.it.

Bar Mocambo

Bar Mocambo, at Via San Bernardo 29, Pisa, +39 339 31 08 164, provides a cozy atmosphere with books and comfortable chairs, where guests enjoy cocktails and snacks while the owner mingles.

Borderline Club

Borderline Club, Via Giuseppe Vernaccini 7, Pisa, +39 366 487 3312, features live music weekly, including jam sessions on Mondays, Italian and international concerts on Thursdays, and disco rock on weekends.

Boccaccio Club

Boccaccio Club, Centro Torretta White, Via Del Tiglio 149, Calcinaia, +39 0587 2970, offers five dance floors and six themed rooms with various music genres. Visit www.boccaccio.it or email info@boccaccio.it for more information.

Barrique

Located at Via Domenico Cavalca 7, Pisa, +39 349 239 3604, Barrique is a genuine wine bar offering a lively atmosphere, great cocktails, and food in Tuscany's renowned wine region.

Cafè Albatross

Cafè Albatross, Via Domenico Cavalca 64, Pisa, features a rock bar vibe with live concerts and cold beers, perfect for alternative music fans. Happy hour is from 7 PM to 8 PM.

ELEVEN CAFÉ

ELEVEN CAFÉ excels in negronis despite its name suggesting coffee, serving high-quality cocktails in a relaxed setting. Aperitivo hour starts around 7 PM.

Skyline American Bar

Skyline American Bar offers affordable tapas and cocktails with a New York ambiance and stunning Pisa views, transitioning from café to cocktail bar after sunset.

Shopping in Pisa

The area surrounding the Leaning Tower of Pisa is inundated with generic souvenir shops. Instead, head to Corso Italia and Borgo Stretto for a more authentic shopping experience. Corso Italia features affordable, everyday Italian fashion, while Borgo Stretto houses upscale boutiques in a medieval setting.

Additionally, Via Mercanti and Via dei Rigattieri offer a range of high-quality shops, and throughout the city center, you can find vendors selling rare books and artworks.

For antique enthusiasts, the Antique and Handicraft Fair is a must-visit, held on the second weekend of each month (excluding July and August) across various streets including Via Santa Maria, Piazza Felice Cavallotti, Via dei Mille, Via Corsica, Piazza dei Cavalieri, and Via Ulisse Dini.

Lastly, the Mercato delle Vettovaglie, a historic fruit and food market located in its namesake square, operates from Monday to Friday and is well worth a visit for its rich history and local produce.

Other Shopping Spots

Shop at the Leaning Tower of Pisa

The area around the Leaning Tower of Pisa is filled with vendors selling replicas of the iconic structure. Purchase a souvenir for yourself or as a gift, and compare prices to get the best deal.

Antiques Market in Piazza dei Cavalieri

The Antiques Market in Piazza dei Cavalieri is renowned for antiques and is held every second weekend of the month, excluding July and August. It's a prime spot for finding unique items.

Antique & Craft Fairs

Antique and Craft Fairs occur around the city center, including Via Santa Maria and Piazza dei Cavalieri, every second weekend of the month (except July and August). Over 100 artisans showcase their works at these events.

Mercato delle Vettovaglie

Mercato delle Vettovaglie, in Piazza delle Vettovaglie, operates Monday to Friday and is a popular spot for local fruit and food shopping, offering a glimpse into everyday life in Pisa.

Valenti

Established in the 1970s, Valenti is a premier fashion boutique in Pisa, offering high-end brands like Valentino, Burberry, and Prada. Locations include Borgo Stretto 28, 41, 42, 51, and Via Guglielmo Oberdan 6. Visit www.valentipisa.it or call +39 050 97 02 68.

Enoteca Bacchus

Enoteca Bacchus, located at Via Pietro Mascagni 1, is a family-run wine shop specializing in premium wines, rums, and whiskies, with a restaurant at Via Aurelia Sud 8. For more details, visit www.bacchusenoteca.com or call +39 050 50 05 60.

Sanantonio42

Sanantonio42, at Via San Paolo 1, caters to vintage enthusiasts with streetwear, vinyl records, skateboards, and graffiti supplies. Check out www.sanantonio42.it or call +39 050 442 61.

Sergio Capone

Sergio Capone, the exclusive Rolex dealer in Pisa, offers luxury watches and jewelry at Borgo Stretto 6. Explore their collection online at www.sergiocapone.com or call +39 050 971 14 08.

Max il Cuoiaio

Located near Piazza dei Cavalieri, Max il Cuoiaio offers high-quality handmade leather items such as bags, wallets, and belts. For unique gifts away from tourist traps, visit the store.

BB Maison

BB Maison features designer brands like Stuart Weitzman and Repetto, focusing on elegant clothing, accessories, and exclusive perfumes. Visit their website for more information, https://bbmaison.it/

Marina di Pisa Market

Explore the Marina di Pisa market for vintage finds and second-hand goods, set against the backdrop of the Tyrrhenian Sea.

Colline Toscane

Inside Pisa Airport, Colline Toscane offers a range of Italian food and wine products, perfect for last-minute souvenirs.

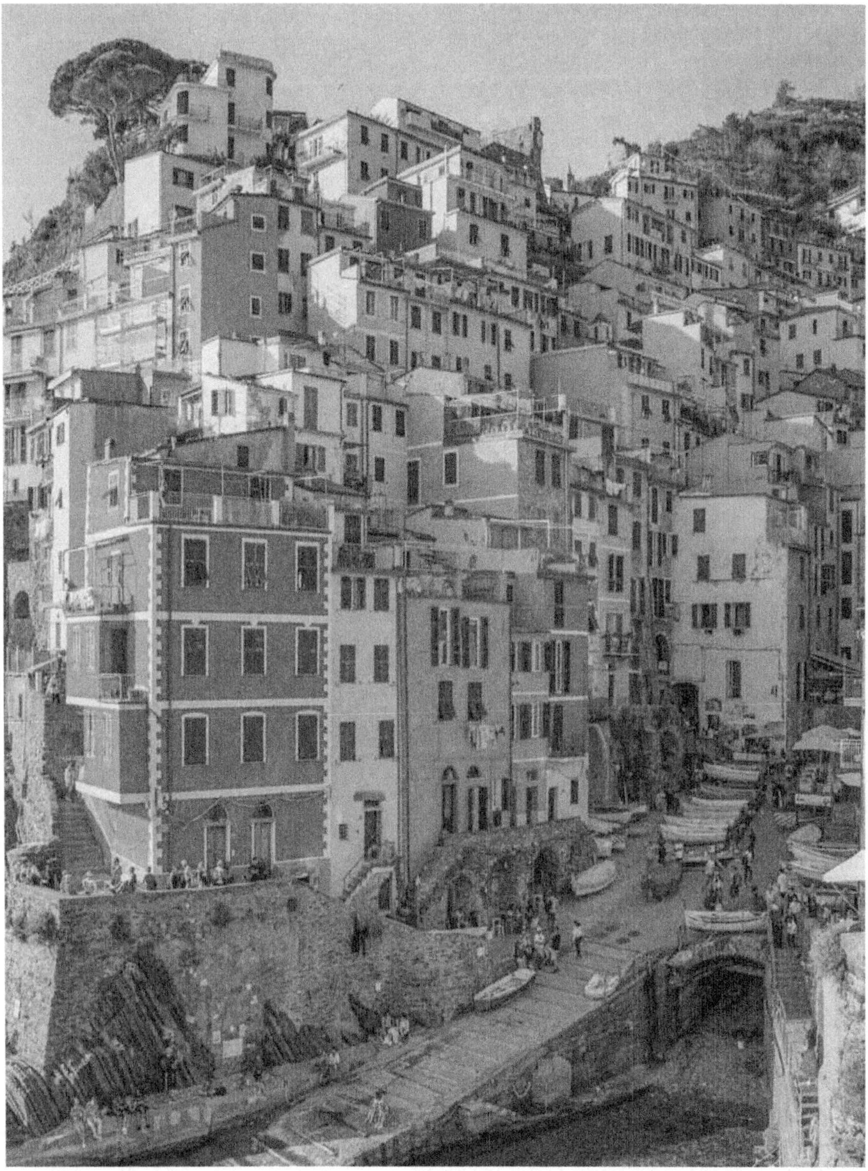

CHAPTER 8
DAY TRIPS FROM PISA

Cinque Terre

A day trip from Pisa to the picturesque seaside of Cinque Terre offers a delightful escape. Comprised of five vibrant fishing villages—Monterosso, Vernazza, Corniglia, Manarola, and Riomaggiore—Cinque Terre boasts colorful buildings, charming eateries, and bustling streets, especially during summer. Visitors can hike the scenic trails linking these villages, though it's wise to check for trail closures due to mudslides. Besides hiking, a ferry services four of the villages, and a train conveniently connects all five, with just minutes between each stop.

To get there by train, travel from Pisa Centrale to any Cinque Terre village with one transfer at La Spezia, where you'll board a regional train. The journey to Monterosso takes approximately 1.25 to 2 hours, depending on the train schedule. For those planning to hike, be sure to check current trail conditions before your trip.

Things to Do in Cinque Terre

Explore Riomaggiore

Riomaggiore, with its charming harbor and pastel-colored houses reflecting Ligurian tradition, is an ideal spot for sunset views in the Cinque Terre. Follow a narrow path from the marina to a rocky beach with crystal-clear waters. After a swim, stroll up the main street. This destination is perfect for young travelers or couples seeking romance. As the sun sets, people gather on the rocks by the harbor to watch the sunset, and numerous restaurants and bars remain open until 1 AM. Nearby, romantic Airbnbs with sea views enhance the experience.

Kayak Adventures

When the waters are calm and warm, renting a kayak or canoe in Riomaggiore offers a peaceful escape from the crowds. Paddle through the Marine Protected Area along the Cinque Terre coastline, exploring caves and deserted beaches. Paddle from Riomaggiore to Manarola and Vernazza to enjoy stunning views of the villages from the sea. Organized kayak tours from Monterosso include guided paddling along the coast towards Vernazza and Guvano beach, with stops for snorkeling. Evening tours with wine and snacks at sunset are available for all skill levels, with necessary equipment provided.

Hike from Volastra to Corniglia

Hiking enthusiasts will appreciate the trails connecting the Cinque Terre villages. One recommended hike is from Volastra to Corniglia, starting with a minibus ride from Manarola to Volastra. This challenging hike along narrow trails through terraced vineyards offers stunning ocean views, highland vineyards, and quaint villages. The hike, taking around two hours, includes a scenic bar stop and a forested section providing relief from the summer heat. Ensure you have proper footwear, water, and sunscreen for this rewarding adventure.

Explore Corniglia

Corniglia is unique among the Cinque Terre villages as it is not directly by the sea but perched atop a rocky promontory over a hundred meters high. Surrounded by vineyards on typical Ligurian terraces, Corniglia offers a quieter experience with fewer tourists. To reach it, you must climb the Lardarina (377 steps) or take a shuttle bus from the train station since it cannot be accessed by sea. The village's narrow streets and pastel-colored houses add to its charm, making it a peaceful retreat with stunning sea views from various high-quality hotels. Despite its tranquility, Corniglia has bars and restaurants but lacks a vibrant nightlife.

Nessun Dorma in Manarola

Manarola, one of the most picturesque Cinque Terre villages, is set on a steep promontory of dark rock, featuring a small port and colorful houses. After a hike, cool off with a swim in the ocean or watch the cliff jumpers at the harbor. For a romantic sunset experience, visit Nessun Dorma bar, which offers stunning views of Manarola. Enjoy their specialties like bruschetta tricolore, mixed cheese and meat platters, or melon with prosciutto. Download the Nessun Dorma app to queue for your table while exploring the town. Manarola also offers beautiful Airbnbs with sea views, ideal for groups or families.

Discover the Coast by Boat

A boat trip is an excellent way to explore the rugged cliffs, turquoise waters, and colorful villages of the Cinque Terre coastline. Ferries run frequently from La Spezia, Portovenere, and Levanto to the Cinque Terre from late March to November 1. Note that ferries do not stop in Corniglia due to its lack of water access. For more details on schedules and prices, visit the Boat Excursions website. A one-day or half-day ticket allows unlimited boat travel and the opportunity to visit Portovenere, a hidden gem near La Spezia.

In Portovenere, stroll through the old town and enjoy views of Palmaria Island from the castle, and don't miss the Bajeicò pesto shop. Alternatively, private boat tours from Monterosso offer a more exclusive experience, with opportunities for swimming and enjoying aperitivo on board.

Enjoy a Beach Day in Monterosso

Monterosso, the largest of the Cinque Terre villages, boasts a long sandy beach located in the newer part of the village, right in front of the station. Here, you can rent sunbeds, umbrellas, and SUP boards. Towards the statue of the Giant at the beach's end, there is a public area with crystal-clear waters. The promenade is lined with restaurants, pubs, and ice-cream shops. On Thursday mornings, you can explore the local market in the town center. The Old Town, with its narrow streets and old fishermen's houses, offers charming bars and seafood restaurants.

Monterosso has several delightful hotels near the beach and beautiful farmhouses surrounded by vineyards and lemon trees in Cinque Terre National Park. For families or groups, there are excellent apartment options available.

Trek from Monterosso to Vernazza

If you have the time, hiking one of the renowned trails between the villages is a must. You'll need a Cinque Terre Trekking Card, which costs €7.50 for one day. Alternatively, the Cinque Terre Treno MS Card allows unlimited train travel between the five towns and access to the trails. For detailed pricing, visit the Cinque Terre Card page. The footpath to Vernazza starts from the eastern part of Monterosso's old town. Follow the pedestrian road to the 4-star Hotel Porto Roca, where the trail begins with a long staircase through vineyards and citrus orchards, offering stunning sea views. You'll pass an antique stone bridge worth a photo stop. As the trail descends, the breathtaking view of Vernazza appears. The path ends in Vernazza's small harbor, perfect for a swim in its natural waters. The trail can be crowded during peak season, so start early to avoid crowds and midday heat. The best months for hiking are March, April, May, June, September, or October when temperatures are milder.

Explore Vernazza in the Afternoon

Vernazza, renowned as one of the most picturesque villages in the Cinque Terre and Italy, centers around a charming piazza with vividly painted houses and a small harbor filled with fishermen's boats. For a delightful lunch, choose one of the local seafood restaurants surrounding the square. The town is best accessed by boat or train, offering scenic travel options.

To capture the quintessential view of Vernazza, hike up the surrounding mountains. Following paths toward Monterosso or Corniglia for about 15 minutes will lead you to renowned photo spots with panoramic vistas of Vernazza, its medieval towers, and the harbor. For an additional fee, you can also climb the Doria Tower for a splendid view.

The streets of Vernazza are lined with bars and gelaterias, such as Gelateria Vernazza, which offers a variety of delicious ice cream flavors. If time permits, relax on the cliffs by the harbor for sunbathing. Accommodation in Vernazza is limited to a few small hotels and romantic Airbnbs, all providing exceptional views of the main square and the vibrant harbor.

Where to Eat

Fuori Rotta, Riomaggiore

Fuori Rotta offers contemporary takes on Cinque Terre cuisine with dishes like "mosaic of vegetables" and calamari stuffed with shellfish and ricotta. Set on a terrace with panoramic views of Riomaggiore, it combines modern flair with traditional flavors.

Visit https://www.ristorantefuorirotta.com/ for more information.

Cecio, Corniglia

Cecio, perched between Corniglia and the Sentiero Azzuro trail, provides hearty traditional meals like marinated anchovies and seafood risotto. Known for its excellent fish soup, it's ideal for hikers needing a substantial meal before or after their trek. Visit http://www.cecio5terre.com/ for more information.

Nessun Dorma, Manarola

Nessun Dorma, located on a cliff in Manarola, is famed for its sunset views and aperitivo hour. Enjoy platters of local anchovies, bruschetta, and salads, while appreciating the beautiful coastal scenery. Note that it doesn't offer pasta or pizza. Visit https://www.nessundormacinqueterre.com/ for more information.

Dau Cila, Riomaggiore

Dau Cila, overlooking Riomaggiore's harbor, serves freshly caught local seafood like grilled octopus and spaghetti with anchovies. Its menu features a selection of local wines, emphasizing the freshest fish from the nearby waters. Call +39 0187 760032

Cappun Magru, Manarola

Cappun Magru in Manarola serves a standout cold seafood and vegetable dish ideal for a seaside lunch, alongside inventive panini and a fine wine selection curated by sommelier Christiana. The restaurant operates for breakfast, lunch, and aperitivo, closing at 6pm. Call +39 0187 760057

Gianni Franzi, Vernazza

Gianni Franzi, located on Vernazza's harbor, offers traditional Cinque Terre fare, including stuffed anchovies and fish ravioli, with the tegame Vernazza, a layered anchovy stew, as a highlight. Visit https://linktr.ee/giannifranzi for more information.

Ciak, Monterosso

Ciak in Monterosso's main piazza has been a local favorite for nearly 50 years, serving dishes like octopus salad, grilled fish, and tiramisu in traditional terracotta pots. For more information, visit, http://www.ristoranteciak.net/.

Ristorante La Torre, Vernazza

Ristorante La Torre, perched on the edge of Vernazza, provides stunning sea views and excellent homemade pesto, especially enjoyed with bruschetta, after a hike from the Sentiero Azzuro trail. Call +39 331 883 6610

Lucca

Lucca is situated 14 miles northeast of Pisa and 48 miles west of Florence. For visitors arriving from Rome, it's efficient to explore both Lucca and Pisa in a single day; if possible, consider an overnight stay for a more leisurely experience.

Train Travel Details

- From Florence: The journey takes approximately 1 hour and 20 minutes, with ticket prices ranging from €7.90 to €10.00.
- From Pisa: The trip is about 27 minutes and costs €3.60.
- From Rome: The fastest trains take around 3.5 hours, with fares varying between €27 and €60, depending on the service.

Things to do in Lucca

Stroll Along Lucca's Historic City Walls

Lucca's extensive city walls, dating back to the Renaissance, are a key feature of the town, preserving its independence until the 19th century. Visitors can walk along these historic ramparts, enjoying panoramic views of the city and changing seasonal colors. The walls offer a unique vantage point to appreciate the city's landscape and architectural beauty.

Visit the Volto Santo at Lucca's Cathedral

Inside the Cathedral of San Martino in Lucca, the Volto Santo, or "Holy Face," is an ancient wooden crucifix with a rich history of legends and devotion. Located in the white marble 'tempietto' within the cathedral's right nave, this artifact is central to the Luminara di Santa Croce festival held every September.

The distinctive appearance of the crucifix, including Christ's long tunic and open eyes, symbolizes victory over death, reflecting centuries of pilgrimage and reverence. Visit http://www.museocattedralelucca.it/, for more information.

Relax in Piazza Anfiteatro

Piazza Anfiteatro, originally a Roman amphitheater, maintains its distinctive oval shape, and the surrounding buildings incorporate stones from the ancient structure. This central square is a popular destination for enjoying drinks and coffee at its open-air cafes. Historically a venue for lively Roman spectacles, today it serves as a vibrant spot for socializing with aperitifs and cappuccinos.

Ascend the Guinigi Tower

The Guinigi Tower, a 14th-century landmark in Lucca, features a unique rooftop garden of holm oaks, a remnant of the Guinigi family's influence. The tower provides sweeping 360-degree views of Lucca from its green summit.

For an additional historical experience, visit the Torre delle Ore on Via Fillungo, which, with its 207 steps, offers another panoramic view of the city.

Zuppa di Farro and Buccellato

Sampling local dishes is a must when exploring Italian towns, and Lucca is no exception with its unique culinary offerings. Be sure to try the zuppa di farro, a robust soup featuring spelt, a staple in Lucchese cuisine. Additionally, indulge in buccellato, Lucca's traditional aniseed-flavored cake. Pasticceria Taddeucci, located in the scenic Piazza San Michele, is renowned for this delightful treat.

Shop Along Via Fillungo

Via Fillungo is Lucca's bustling main street, nestled in the historic center. This charming, narrow street is lined with elegant boutiques, bakeries, and gelaterias, making it a prime spot for shopping. Whether you're hunting for stylish clothing and shoes or savoring sweet treats at one of the pasticcerie, Via Fillungo offers a delightful experience and excellent opportunities for people-watching.

Saint Zita at San Frediano Church

In Lucca, often called the 'town of 100 churches,' the Romanesque Church of San Frediano stands out as a must-visit. Here, you can encounter the mummified body of Saint Zita, displayed in a glass case.

Saint Zita, the patron saint of maidens and domestic workers, lived in Lucca and was known for her miracles, humility, and perseverance despite mistreatment. After her death, her body remained remarkably preserved, leading to her canonization in 1696. The church, with its rich history and connection to Saint Zita, offers a unique glimpse into Lucca's religious heritage. Contact +39 349 8440290 for more information.

Giacomo Puccini's Home and Villa

Giacomo Puccini, the renowned Italian composer known for operas like *La Bohème* and *Madame Butterfly*, was born in Lucca in 1858. You can visit his birthplace in Piazza Cittadella, marked by a bronze statue. For a deeper dive into Puccini's life, travel to Torre del Lago Puccini, just 30 minutes from Lucca. Here, his villa overlooks the scenic Massaciuccoli Lake, offering insights into his life and work. The villa, still owned by the Puccini family, features his piano and has been meticulously restored, allowing visitors to experience the ambiance where his iconic melodies were created.

What to Eat

Testaroli Pasta

Testaroli pasta, believed to be the earliest form of pasta, dates back to the Etruscans who first settled in modern-day Tuscany thousands of years ago. Unlike traditional pasta, which is boiled, testaroli is made from a batter poured onto a hot surface called "testo." This thin, spongy pasta is cut into diamond or rectangular shapes and typically served with pesto.

Tordelli Lucchesi

Tordelli Lucchesi, a specialty of Lucca, is a semicircular pasta similar to ravioli. These delicate pasta pockets are filled with a mixture of pork, wild boar, or beef, along with Swiss chard, pine nuts, raisins, spices, and cheese. They are served with a rich ragù sauce made from pancetta, soffritto (a blend of onion, carrot, and celery), and occasionally beef and pork, seasoned with sage, nutmeg, and red wine.

Cantucci e Vin Santo

Cantucci, resembling the American-Italian "biscotti," are small, crunchy almond cookies originating from Prato, just 20 minutes east of Lucca. These cookies have become a staple throughout Tuscany, including Lucca. Traditionally, they are served with vin santo, a sweet, golden fortified dessert wine. The correct way to enjoy this treat is by dipping the cantucci into the vin santo before taking a bite, allowing the flavors to meld perfectly.

Where to Eat

Sotto Sotto Ristorantino

Sotto Sotto Ristorantino offers local Lucchese specialties like bean and farro soup, tortelli Lucchesi, and testaroli, with prices for pasta dishes under 15 euros and meat dishes around 20 euros. Reservations are recommended due to limited seating. Location: Piazza dell'Anfiteatro, 1, 55100 Lucca.

Ristorante Giglio

Ristorante Giglio, a fine dining spot with a Michelin star, offers a mix of classic and contemporary Italian dishes, an impressive wine list, and a charming atmosphere with frescoed ceilings. Located at Piazza del Giglio, 2, 55100 Lucca.

L'Angolo Tondo

L'Angolo Tondo, in Piazza dell'Anfiteatro, 51, 55100 Lucca, serves traditional Lucchese food using local ingredients, including a unique take on the classic Tuscan dessert cantucci e vin santo. The interior blends modern elegance with nostalgic charm.

Funiculì Pizzeria

Funiculì Pizzeria, located at Viale S. Concordio, 483, 55100 Lucca, serves traditional Neapolitan pizza with local ingredients, including seafood. Expect to spend under 10 euros per pizza in this locals-favored spot.

Buca di Sant'Antonio

Buca di Sant'Antonio, Via della Cervia, 3, 55100 Lucca, offers traditional Lucchese pasta dishes like tordelli Lucchesi in a 241-year-old setting with an extensive wine list, just a 3-minute walk from Lucca's clock tower.

Florence

Traveling from Pisa to Florence is straightforward, given the high demand for this popular route between two major Tuscan destinations. Various transportation options are available, including buses, trains, cars, and planes.

By Plane

Tuscany is served by two main airports: Pisa's International Galileo Galilei Airport, just one kilometer from the city center, and Florence's Amerigo Vespucci Airport, located about four kilometers from Florence's center. The latter primarily handles domestic flights. Flying from Pisa to Florence is quick, with efficient connections to and from the airports. From Pisa, you can reach the airport by bus, train, or car. Upon landing at Amerigo Vespucci Airport, passengers can easily travel to central Florence via a bus service to the Santa Maria Novella train station, or by taxi or rental car, typically taking 15 to 20 minutes.

By Bus

Traveling from Pisa to Florence by bus is another efficient option. The primary bus operator, CPT (Compagnia Pisana Transporti), departs from Piazza Vittorio Emanuele II, near Pisa's Central Station. Alternatively, you can catch a bus directly from Pisa's International Airport, which offers a variety of transfer services. Terravision buses provide a convenient and quick connection to Florence, stopping at the Santa Maria Novella station in the city center. For schedule details, tickets can be purchased at the Information Desk or online at [pisa-airport.com](http://www.pisa-airport.com).

By Train

Traveling from Pisa to Florence by train is a convenient and popular method in Tuscany. One option is to take a train directly from Pisa International Airport, with five trains running daily between the two cities. For more details, visit [pisa-airport.com]). Alternatively, you can board a train from Pisa Central Station or the smaller San Rossore Station. Approximately 40 trains operate daily, covering the distance in about 90 minutes, reflecting the high demand between these tourist hubs.

By Car

Driving from Pisa to Florence offers flexibility and scenic views. To embark on this journey, follow SS1 Aurelia, the main road leading out of Pisa, then merge onto either the A11 Mare-Florence motorway or the Pisa-Livorno-Florence expressway. Renting a car provides an opportunity to explore the Tuscan countryside at your own pace.

Things to do in Florence

Cathedral of Santa Maria del Fiore and Piazza Duomo

Piazza Duomo, encompassing the Cathedral of Santa Maria del Fiore and its related buildings, houses some of Italy's most significant artistic and architectural masterpieces. This complex includes the cathedral itself, the baptistery, the bell tower, and the cathedral museum, showcasing works by Renaissance giants like Ghiberti, Brunelleschi, Donatello, Giotto, and Michelangelo.

You can admire the intricately decorated marble facades and explore the stained-glass artworks inside. To avoid long lines, consider booking the "Skip the Line: Florence Duomo with Brunelleschi's Dome Climb" tour, which offers a comprehensive 2.5-hour experience including entrance fees and optional museum access. For more details, visit [Florence Duomo Tours](http://www.florence-duomo-tours.com).

Battistero di San Giovanni (Baptistery of St. John)

The 12th-century Baptistery of St. John, or Battistero di San Giovanni, is a masterpiece renowned for its octagonal marble façade and stunning interior mosaics. The highlight is Ghiberti's bronze panels on the main doors, known as the "Gates of Paradise," celebrated for their exceptional craftsmanship. To view these panels up close and explore other artifacts related to the baptistery, visit the Museo dell'Opera del Duomo. For more information on the museum, check [Museo dell'Opera del Duomo](http://www.operaduomo.firenze.it).

See Florence from Piazzale Michelangiolo

Often mistakenly referred to as Piazzale Michelangelo, Piazzale Michelangiolo is a prime viewpoint offering sweeping panoramic vistas of Florence. It is the ideal location for iconic photographs of the city's skyline, including the imposing dome of the cathedral. To avoid the tourist crowds, visit in the late afternoon or early evening, particularly at sunset. From this terrace, you can appreciate the grandeur of Brunelleschi's dome and view landmarks such as the Ponte Vecchio, Palazzo Vecchio, and Santa Croce. You can either walk from the city center, a 30-minute uphill climb, or take bus 12 or 13 for a more comfortable journey. For a fuller experience, consider walking to the nearby San Miniato al Monte church.

Uffizi Palace and Gallery

The Uffizi Gallery stands as one of the world's premier art museums, renowned for its extensive and exceptional collection spanning the 14th to 16th centuries. It offers a profound glimpse into the evolution of Western art, showcasing works from Byzantine to Renaissance masters. The building, originally a Medici palace, was designed to accommodate governmental offices and the family's art collection. Highlights include the Tribuna, an octagonal room dedicated to Francesco I de' Medici's prized artworks. To bypass long queues, opt for the "Skip the Line: Florence Accademia and Uffizi Gallery Tour," which provides priority access and a guided tour. For more information, visit [Uffizi Gallery](https://www.uffizi.it).

Piazza della Signoria and the Loggia dei Lanzi

Piazza della Signoria has been Florence's political hub since the 14th century, with Etruscan and Roman artifacts discovered beneath its surface. Today, it remains a vibrant social space where locals and tourists gather. The square features the Neptune Fountain and the Palazzo Vecchio, which continues to serve as the city's government seat. By night, the illuminated fountain and surrounding architecture create a pleasant ambiance, complemented by nearby restaurants with outdoor seating. The Loggia dei Lanzi, adjacent to the Uffizi Gallery, is an open-air sculpture gallery showcasing notable works, including Benvenuto Cellini's "Perseus with the Head of Medusa" and a replica of Michelangelo's "David" positioned in front of the Palazzo Vecchio.

Galleria dell'Accademia (Academy Gallery)

The Galleria dell'Accademia is renowned for housing Michelangelo's original statue of "David," which is now protected by glass following an attack. This gallery also features Michelangelo's unfinished sculptures, including the "Four Slaves," and his incomplete "St. Matthew" intended for Florence Cathedral. In addition to Michelangelo's works, the gallery displays significant pieces by Florentine artists from the 13th to 16th centuries, such as Sandro Botticelli's "Madonna." To avoid lengthy waits, consider the "Skip the Line: Florence Accademia and Uffizi Gallery Tour," offering priority access and a guided experience. For more details, visit [Galleria dell'Accademia](https://www.accademia.org).

San Lorenzo and Michelangelo's Medici Tombs

San Lorenzo, the Medici family's chosen church, showcases the work of renowned Renaissance artists. Designed by Filippo Brunelleschi, the church reflects his architectural genius, though his death prevented him from completing the project. Michelangelo, tasked with creating the Medici tombs in the New Sacristy, also left his work unfinished due to his passing. Despite this, the existing sculptures are acclaimed as masterpieces of marble artistry. Visitors to San Lorenzo will encounter significant Renaissance works in the Old Sacristy, New Sacristy, Princes' Chapel, and the Laurenziana Library, with contributions from artists such as Donatello and Sandro Botticelli.

Palazzo Vecchio (Palazzo della Signoria)

Palazzo Vecchio, located on Piazza della Signoria, is a monumental symbol of Florence's history and power. This fortress-like building once served as the seat of the city's government and the residence of the influential Medici family. The opulent interiors and grand galleries, decorated by the era's top artists, reflect the city's historical and political significance. Visitors should take advantage of free tours to explore secret passages used by the Medici family and visit the roof in the evening for panoramic views of Florence. For further information and tour schedules, visit the [Palazzo Vecchio website](https://www.palazzovecchio-museum.com).

Santa Croce

Santa Croce is not only an architectural marvel with its Tuscan marble façade but also a mausoleum housing some of Florence's most illustrious figures. The church features significant Renaissance art, including Giotto's frescoes in the Cappella Bardi and Cappella Peruzzi, which influenced artists like Masaccio and Michelangelo. Donatello's "Christ Crucified" and Taddeo Gaddi's frescoes in the Cappella Baroncelli further enhance the church's artistic importance. The most notable piece is Cimabue's "Crucifix," pivotal in transitioning from Byzantine stiffness to Renaissance naturalism. The nave contains the tombs of prominent individuals such as Michelangelo, Galileo, and Machiavelli. For more information, visit [Santa Croce](https://www.santacroceopera.it).

Ponte Vecchio

The Ponte Vecchio stands as one of Florence's most iconic landmarks, known for its distinctive design featuring a row of shops perched above the arches of the bridge. Historically, these shops housed skilled goldsmiths, and today, they still offer a captivating selection of jewelry. However, many visitors miss the hidden gem above—the Corridoio Vasariano (Vasari Corridor). This passageway was constructed by the architect Giorgio Vasari to connect the Medici's offices in Palazzo Vecchio with their residence at the Pitti Palace. The corridor's walls display a priceless collection of portraits by renowned artists including Rembrandt, Leonardo da Vinci, Raphael, Michelangelo, and Velázquez. The bridge's central arches offer views down the Arno River, though it can be crowded, particularly during peak tourist seasons, making it challenging to get a clear view.

Palazzo Pitti (Pitti Palace)

A visit to the Pitti Palace provides a comprehensive experience of Florence's rich offerings, including its extensive art collection, historical significance, and opulent gardens. The palace, originally a Medici residence, houses a remarkable art gallery featuring masterpieces by Raphael, Titian, Rubens, and Tintoretto, displayed within the lavish Royal Apartments. The rooms, designed for grandeur and social gatherings, present artworks in a setting that rivals the Uffizi Gallery. The palace complex also includes museums, showcasing Florentine craftsmanship and royal history, and the Boboli Gardens, one of Italy's premier green spaces. For more details, visit the [Palazzo Pitti website](https://www.uffizi.it/en/pitti-palace).

Santa Maria Novella

Santa Maria Novella, a Dominican church with a striking striped marble façade, offers a distinctive architectural style among Florence's churches. The façade features elegant curves, imitation windows, and intricate arches. Inside, the church is adorned with some of the city's finest frescoes by masters such as Masaccio, Giotto, Domenico Ghirlandaio, Lippi, and Paolo Uccello. The highlight includes the Chapel of the Rucellai, decorated with Andrea di Bonaiuto's notable 14th-century frescoes. The church also houses Brunelleschi's marble pulpit and wooden crucifix, Vasari's Rosary Madonna, and a bronze by Lorenzo Ghiberti. Additionally, visitors can explore the historic pharmacy of the convent, offering herbal remedies and floral lotions.

For further information, visit the [Santa Maria Novella website](https://www.santamarianovella.it).

San Miniato al Monte

San Miniato al Monte stands out with its striking green-and-white marble façade, visible after a short walk from Piazzale Michelangiolo or via a direct bus ride. This church is notable for introducing the dramatic façade style to Florence, featuring a gold mosaic and a design influenced by Classical Roman and Byzantine art. Inside, visitors encounter a spacious nave with a mosaic floor and a painted wooden ceiling, leading to a splendid Renaissance chapel beneath a glazed blue-and-white terracotta ceiling. Highlights include Byzantine-style mosaics, a 12th-century marble pulpit, and an elaborately decorated choir screen. The sacristy is especially impressive, adorned with Spinello Aretino's vibrant 14th-century frescoes depicting the Life of St. Benedict. The church is located at Via delle Porte Sante, 34, Florence.

Bargello Palace National Museum

The Bargello Palace, home to a collection of Michelangelo's masterpieces, is a must-visit for art enthusiasts. This museum showcases an extensive array of works by renowned artists such as Donatello, the della Robbias, Cellini, Brunelleschi, and Ghiberti, spanning from the 14th to the 16th centuries. In addition to sculptures, the museum features a notable collection of ivory carvings, majolica, and Renaissance enamels and gold work. The emphasis on decorative arts and sculpture distinguishes the Bargello from other Florentine museums. The museum is located at Via del Proconsolo 4, Florence.

Explore the Boboli Gardens

The Boboli Gardens, situated behind the Pitti Palace, extend over 111 acres of meticulously manicured terraces. Established between 1550 and 1560 by Grand Duke Cosimo I, these gardens have influenced royal garden designs across Europe, including the famous gardens at Versailles. The gardens feature various fountains, statues, and the Grotta del Buontalenti, a faux cave with intricately carved stalactites and stalagmites. Visitors can also explore a maze, formal garden beds, and an amphitheater set in an old quarry. The highest point offers views from the Kaffeehaus terrace, and the Casino del Cavaliere at the top of the hill displays a rich collection of porcelains owned by the Medici and Savoy families.

Oltrarno District and Piazza Santo Spirito

Exploring the Oltrarno district offers a glimpse into the heart of Florence's artisan community. The narrow, atmospheric streets are home to workshops specializing in traditional crafts such as woodwork, silver and goldsmithing, gilding, miniature mosaics, decorative papers, and leather bookbinding. Visitors will find a variety of unique items for sale, perfect for souvenirs or gifts, including finely bound journals and intricately gilded wooden boxes.

After wandering through the Oltrarno, take a moment to relax in Piazza Santo Spirito. This charming square is less crowded and offers a more intimate atmosphere compared to the larger, busier squares across the river. Find a spot at a local café or restaurant to enjoy the vibrant market scene or watch local children playing. The Basilica of Santo Spirito, located in the square, might not be as renowned as other churches in Florence, but it is a prime example of Renaissance architecture and houses significant artworks, especially in its transept chapels.

Palazzo Medici-Riccardi

The Palazzo Medici-Riccardi, completed in 1464, presents a more understated elegance compared to the later opulent residences of the Medici family. It served as the Medici residence for nearly a century until Cosimo I relocated to the Palazzo Vecchio. The palace features a well-preserved staircase leading to the Palace Chapel, which is adorned with frescoes by Benozzo Gozzoli depicting 15th-century Florentine court life. Despite modifications made by the Riccardi family, who succeeded the Medicis, the Medici Museum on the ground floor maintains the original interior. One notable highlight is Filippo Lippi's "Madonna and Child," painted in 1442. The Palazzo Medici-Riccardi is located at Via Cavour 1 & 3, Florence. For more details, visit [www.palazzo-medici.it]

Mercato Centrale

To immerse yourself in local life, head to Mercato Centrale, Florence's bustling food market. While the approach may lead you past various street vendors selling mass-produced goods, the market itself is a sensory delight filled with the aromas of fresh herbs, flowers, and produce. Inside, you'll mingle with locals shopping for daily groceries and discover a range of

Tuscan delicacies including fine olive oils, olives, candied fruits, and nougat.

The upper floor features a food court, ideal for a quick and tasty lunch. Mercato Centrale is located at Piazza del Mercato, Florence.

Bardini Museum and Gardens

In the late 1800s, art collector Stefano Bardini transformed a collection of buildings on a hillside in the Oltrarno district into a museum and garden. He meticulously repurposed architectural elements from demolished medieval and Renaissance structures, integrating monumental fireplaces, doors, columns, and ceilings into his eclectic home. This unique setting now houses Bardini's vast collection of art and antiques.

Adjacent to the museum, Bardini acquired and developed a garden into an open-air gallery for displaying his sculptures. The Bardini Gardens offer stunning views of Florence and provide a serene escape from the city's hustle. The garden is particularly enchanting in April when vibrant wisteria adorns the pergola. Visitors can enjoy the lush greenery, mosaic fountains, and an English-style garden. The terrace features a café, enhancing the garden's appeal as a relaxation spot. Note that the garden and museum require separate admission. The Bardini Gardens are located at Costa San Giorgio 2, Florence, and the Bardini Museum is at Via dei Renai 37, Florence.

Brancacci Chapel

Hidden behind the unassuming facade of Santa Maria del Carmine church, the Brancacci Chapel is home to some of the most significant frescoes of the 15th century. The chapel's walls and ceilings showcase scenes from the life of St. Peter and Old Testament stories, painted by Masaccio and Masolino, two leading artists of the early Renaissance. Their works are noted for their innovative use of perspective and vibrant color, which bring a dynamic and expressive quality to their figures.

Masaccio, a pivotal figure in the Italian Renaissance, is renowned for his contributions to the Quattrocento period, and his frescoes in the Brancacci Chapel are among his most celebrated achievements. The chapel was later completed in the 1400s by Filippino Lippi, adding to its historical and artistic significance. Despite its importance, the Brancacci Chapel remains one of Florence's lesser-known treasures. It is located at Piazza del Carmine 14, Florence.

Museo Galileo

Florence's rich tapestry of Renaissance art often overshadows the era's contributions to science. The Museo Galileo highlights this crucial aspect of the Renaissance, showcasing the intersection of art and science. This museum presents an impressive collection of scientific instruments from the Renaissance period, including Galileo Galilei's own tools. The exhibits feature intricate astronomical, navigational, and surveying instruments crafted from metal, wood, and gold. These artifacts illustrate the period's innovative spirit and the connection between scientific exploration and artistic craftsmanship. For more details, visit the museum at Piazza dei Giudici 1, Florence, or check their website at [Museo Galileo](https://www.museogalileo.it/en/).

Piazza Santa Croce

Piazza Santa Croce remains a focal point for high-quality Florentine leather goods, continuing a tradition dating back to the Renaissance. The area, historically home to leather workshops and tanneries, still offers some of the best leather products in Florence. For authentic, well-crafted leather items, visit the Scuola di Cuoio, located within the cloister of Santa Croce. This leatherworking school not only produces exquisite handmade leather products such as wallets, handbags, and jackets but also offers a glimpse into the craft process.

Francesca Gori's exclusive handbags, crafted from rare and exotic leathers, are available here. Other items include luggage, bound books, belts, and leather clothing.

Additionally, Misuri, situated in a frescoed former palazzo on Piazza Santa Croce, offers high-quality traditional leather goods. For more information, visit the Scuola di Cuoio at Piazza Santa Croce, Florence, or explore their offerings online at [Scuola di Cuoio](http://www.scuoladelcuoio.com).

Where to Eat

Club Culinario da Osvaldo

At Piazza dei Peruzzi, 3/r, Florence, Club Culinario da Osvaldo offers Tuscan comfort food in a rustic villa setting. Expect hearty dishes like potato tortelli, roasted squab, and local fish stews, with desserts like tiramisu and Sardinian seada. Visit their website at clubosvaldo.com.

Vini e Vecchi Sapori

Located at Via dei Magazzini, 3/r, Florence, Vini e Vecchi Sapori is a lively trattoria near Piazza della Signoria, serving classics like fried courgette flowers and saffron cream pasta. For more details, check their Facebook page or call +39 055 293045.

Il Vecchio e Il Mare

Find Il Vecchio e Il Mare at Via Vincenzo Gioberti, 61N, Florence, offering Neapolitan-style pizzas and seafood with a relaxed atmosphere. Enjoy unique ingredients like Bronte pistachios and truffles. Visit [ilvecchioeilmare.com] for more info.

Cibreo

Cibreo, located at Via de' Macci, 122r, Florence, is renowned for its refined Tuscan cuisine and variety of dining experiences. Try their stuffed meats, seafood stews, and flourless chocolate cake. Explore more at cibreo.com.

Essenziale

Located at P.za di Cestello, 3R, Florence, Essenziale offers a blend of traditional Tuscan cuisine and innovative techniques, such as freeze-dried raspberries on saffron risotto. Check their rotating menus at essenziale.me.

Nugolo

Nugolo, found at Via della Mattonaia, 27 R, Florence, highlights Tuscan terroir with a menu focused on garden-sourced ingredients and creative dishes like sea urchin linguine. Discover more at ilnugolo.com.

Zeb

At Via S. Miniato, 2r, Florence, Zeb serves exceptional fresh pasta and meaty ragu, alongside a curated selection of Italian and French wines. Visit zebgastronomia.com for details.

Osteria dell'Enoteca

Osteria dell'Enoteca, located at Via Romana, 70/r, Florence, specializes in steak with a superb wine list and offers dishes like game ragu pasta and cod with chickpeas. Explore their offerings at [osteriadellenoteca.com]

Osteria Tre Panche at Hotel Hermitage

Located at Vicolo Marzio, 1, Florence, this rooftop restaurant features rich, truffle-enhanced classics like taglioni and tortelloni in pecorino fondue. The terrace offers covered seating year-round. Visit [osteriadelletrepanche.com] for more details.

Locale Firenze

Found at Via delle Seggiole, 12r, Florence, Locale Firenze offers creative dining in a historic palace with unique dishes using ingredients like smoked tea and caramelized miso. Enjoy their acclaimed cocktails and tasting menus at [localefirenze.it].

Gucci Osteria

Situated at P.za della Signoria, 10, Florence, Gucci Osteria combines Italian cuisine with Mexican and Japanese influences under the guidance of Karime Lopez and Takahiko Kondo. Start with cocktails at Gucci Giardino before dining; details at gucciosteria.com.

Siena

The city is renowned for its remarkable Gothic structures, including the cathedral and various palaces, all constructed from locally sourced red clay bricks. As you navigate Siena's historic old town, or Centro Storico, be prepared for a lot of walking, often on steep inclines.

While Siena is famously known for the Palio, an exhilarating horse race held twice each summer, the city offers much more.

Wandering through its charming, vehicle-free stone streets, you can experience a genuine sense of medieval Italy.

Traveling from Pisa to Siena

By Bus

You can reach Siena from Pisa by bus in under two hours, with a brief stop in Poggibonsi. Buses depart from Pisa International Airport or Piazza Vittorio Emanuele II, arriving at Piazza Gramsci in Siena, with additional stops at Siena Nord and Siena P. Rosselli. For more details, visit [Pisa Airport](https://www.pisa-airport.com).

By Train

Trains offer a direct route from Pisa to Siena in about 100 minutes. Trains run hourly and the Siena train station, located at Via Carlo Rosselli, is approximately 2 kilometers from the city center.

By Car

Driving from Pisa to Siena takes around two hours. The recommended route involves traveling on SS1 Aurelia, then switching to the A11 Mare-Florence motorway or the Pisa-Livorno-Florence expressway, and continuing south on SS222 Chiantigiana or SS2 Siena-Florence motorway.

Things to do in Siena

Cathedral of Santa Maria Assunta

The Cathedral of Santa Maria Assunta in Siena stands as a prime example of Gothic architecture, shaped significantly by Giovanni Pisano, who designed the façade and crafted many of its statues and reliefs. Its striking façade, with alternating dark and light marble stripes, contrasts with the predominant red brick of Siena's buildings. Inside, the cathedral is a treasure trove of art, featuring works by Nicola and Giovanni Pisano, Donatello, Bernini, Lorenzo Ghiberti, Pinturicchio, and others. Notable highlights include the frescoed Biblioteca Piccolomini, Ghiberti and Donatello's bronze reliefs in the Baptistery of San Giovanni, Nicola Pisano's 13th-century marble pulpit, and the intricately inlaid marble floor. The cathedral complex also encompasses the Museo dell'Opera del Duomo, housing the original stained-glass window, and the Crypt, with its 13th-century wall paintings, accessible through a separate entrance. The Porta del Cielo, offering elevated views of the cathedral nave, requires an additional fee. The Opa Si Pass, valid for three days, covers all attractions except the Porta del Cielo. To maximize your visit and avoid lines, consider the Skip the Line: Siena Duomo and City Walking Tour. Address: Piazza del Duomo 8, Siena Website: (https://operaduomo.siena.it)

Piazza del Campo

Piazza del Campo is the focal point of Siena's historic center, renowned for its striking layout and architectural harmony.

This expansive square is framed by the curving facades of surrounding buildings and is dominated by the elegant Palazzo Pubblico and its tall tower. At the upper end of the square stands the Fonte Gaia, a 15th-century fountain designed by Iácopo della Quercia. The original marble reliefs were relocated to the Museo Civico for preservation, and the current reliefs are precise replicas. The unified aesthetic of the piazza is accentuated by the Palazzo Sansedoni, a notable structure completed between 1216 and 1339, which complements the Palazzo Pubblico's design. Address: Piazza del Campo, Siena

Palazzo Pubblico and Museo Civico

The Palazzo Pubblico, a key feature of Piazza del Campo, was constructed in the late 13th and early 14th centuries. Its facade, a mix of travertine and brick, is distinguished by elegant arches and battlements, with the black and white Balzana emblem of Siena prominently displayed. Inside, the Palazzo houses a collection of frescoes from the Sienese school, including Ambrogio Lorenzetti's famous works on Good and Bad Government in the Sala della Pace. The Sala del Mappamondo features Simone Martini's Maestà, while the adjoining chapel contains frescoes by Taddeo di Bartolo. The Museo Civico, located on the upper floors, showcases Siena's history through Renaissance paintings, silverwork, and original Fonte Gaia sculptures. Address: Piazza del Campo 1, Siena. Website: [Museo Civico Siena](https://www.museocivicosiena.it

Torre del Mangia

The Torre del Mangia, a striking 102-meter tower at one end of the Palazzo Pubblico, is a prime example of medieval architecture. Erected between 1338 and 1348 by Minuccio and Francesco di Rinaldo, this slender brick tower features a battlemented top with travertine supports. You can ascend the several hundred steps to reach the observation platform, which offers panoramic views of Siena and the surrounding Tuscan landscape.

At the base of the tower, the Renaissance-style Cappella di Piazza, constructed in 1352, commemorates Siena's recovery from the plague of 1348. It is recommended to book tickets early and choose a late afternoon time slot for a memorable experience. Address: Piazza del Campo, Siena

Il Palio (Horse Race)

The Palio, Siena's famed horse race, occurs twice each summer on July 2 and August 16, but the event's spirit pervades the city year-round. On race days, the Piazza del Campo becomes the venue for this historic competition, where ten horses and riders race bareback for the silk banner, or pallium. Notably, the race is won by the horse that crosses the finish line first, regardless of the rider's position. The Palio is marked by vibrant parades, flag-throwing displays, and costumed knights, reflecting its origins in the 1500s. Throughout Siena, you'll find banners and souvenirs celebrating the various neighborhood associations, or contradi, involved in the race. Address: Piazza del Campo, Siena. Website: [Il Palio Siena](https://www.ilpalio.it)

Pinacoteca Nazionale (National Gallery)

Housed in the elegant Palazzo Buonsignori, an early 15th-century Late Gothic building, the Pinacoteca Nazionale in Siena showcases a rich collection of Sienese art from the 12th to the 16th centuries. This gallery features works by prominent Siena artists, including Guido da Siena's "Raising of Lazarus" and "Entry into Jerusalem," Duccio di Buoninsegna's "Virgin and Child" and "Madonna dei Francescani," as well as Ambrogio Lorenzetti's "Madonna Enthroned" and "Annunciation." Noteworthy pieces also include Pietro Lorenzetti's "John the Baptist" and "Allegory of Sin and Salvation," and Pinturicchio's "Holy Family." The gallery's floor includes marble inlay cartoons by Beccafumi. Address: Via San Pietro 29, Siena Website:

[Pinacoteca Nazionale](https://www.pinacotecanazionale.siena.it)

The Facciatone

A visit to the Facciatone, the incomplete façade of Siena's cathedral, offers a unique experience. Initiated in the 14th century to expand the cathedral with a new nave, the project was halted due to the plague and economic downturn, leaving only the façade and incomplete sections. Climbing the narrow circular stairs to the top provides breathtaking views of Siena and the Tuscan landscape. This site offers an exceptional vantage point over the cathedral and surrounding areas, though the climb may be challenging for those uneasy with heights.

Address: Piazza del Duomo, Siena. Website:[The Facciatone](https://www.siena.it)

San Doménico

The Church of San Doménico, initially constructed in 1226, is a stark example of Cistercian Gothic architecture. This austere brick edifice was expanded over time, with the addition of the distinctive battlemented campanile in 1340, which contrasts with the original Cistercian style. The interior features a single nave without aisles, a high transept, and an enclosed rectangular choir. The minimalistic design accentuates the church's spaciousness. A notable fresco by Andrea Vanni from around 1400, depicting St. Catherine of Siena, can be seen in a vaulted chapel off the nave. The Cappella di Santa Caterina, located on the nave's right wall, houses two works by Sodoma from 1525: "The Ecstasy of St. Catherine" and "St. Catherine Fainting," alongside a 1446 marble tabernacle by Giovanni di Stefano featuring St. Catherine's head. The high altar displays two angels with a candelabra crafted by Benedetto da Maiano, while side chapels off the choir are adorned with frescoes by Matteo di Giovanni. Beneath the apse, the Fonte Branda, a fountain documented as early as 1081, is located. Address: Piazza San Domenico, Siena

San Francesco

The Gothic Church of San Francesco, initiated by the Franciscan order in 1326 and completed in 1475, mirrors the architectural style of the Mendicant Orders with its aisleless nave and absence of an apse at the eastern end. Like the Church of San Doménico, its campanile was added later, in 1765. Inside, the open timber roof is decorated in alternating black and white bands, reminiscent of the marble of Siena's cathedral, and adorned with banners from historical craft guilds. Noteworthy artworks include a fresco of the Crucifixion by Pietro Lorenzetti, painted around 1330, and frescoes of St. Louis of Toulouse and the Martyrdom of Franciscans at Ceuta by Ambrogio Lorenzetti, located in the left transept. Address: Piazza San Francesco, Siena. Contact +39 0577 49406.

Santa Maria della Scala (Santíssima Annunziata)

The Church of Santa Maria della Scala, also known as Santíssima Annunziata, is located adjacent to the Ospedale di Santa Maria della Scala, directly across from Siena's cathedral. Originally constructed in the late 13th century, the church underwent significant renovations in the late 15th century under the direction of Francesco di Giorgio Martini, who enhanced the apse and coffered ceiling. In 1730, Sebastiano Conca created a prominent fresco for the apse, depicting the Pool of Bethesda and patients awaiting miraculous cures, reflecting the church's historical role as part of a hospital. The high altar features a bronze sculpture of the Risen Christ by Lorenzo Vecchietta, completed in 1476. This piece is a celebrated example of Renaissance art, often compared to Donatello's works.

The adjacent hospital, one of Europe's pioneering institutions and one of the oldest surviving hospitals globally, is now a museum showcasing notable frescoes. Address: Piazza del Duomo 2, Siena Website: [Santa Maria della Scala Museum](https://www.santamariadellascala.com)

Santuario di Santa Caterina

The Santuario di Santa Caterina is a revered site connected to St. Catherine of Siena, a prominent figure in Roman Catholicism. Born to a Siena dyer named Benincasa, Catherine is renowned for her influence in persuading Pope Gregory XI to return from Avignon to Rome in 1377. Among her most celebrated visions was her "mystic marriage" to the Infant Christ, a popular theme in art. Her earliest known portrait, a fresco by Andrea Vanni from around 1400, can be seen in the Church of San Doménico, painted shortly after her death. Her childhood home is now recognized as the Sanctuary of St. Catherine, featuring a striking

Renaissance doorway with the inscription "Sponsae Kristi Catherinae Domus," translating to "House of Catherine, Bride of Christ." Address: Via Santa Caterina, Siena. Website: [Santuario di Santa Caterina](https://www.santacaterina.siena.it)

Santa Maria degli Servi

Situated at the southeastern edge of Siena's historic center, the Church of Santa Maria degli Servi, originally constructed in the 13th century, underwent modifications in the 15th and 16th centuries reflecting the architectural trends of those times. The church features a simplistic facade, left unfinished, while its Romanesque campanile mirrors that of the cathedral with its four-tiered window design, creating a tapering effect. Inside, notable artworks include Coppo di Marcovaldo's *Madonna del Bordone* from 1261 and Pietro Lorenzetti's 14th-century fresco, *Slaughter of the Innocents*, located in the second chapel of the south transept. The high altar displays *Madonna del Popolo*, created by Lippo Memmi around 1317. Nearby, the Porta Romana, a grand gate from 1327, is a significant remnant of the old town's fortifications. Address: Piazza Santa Maria degli Servi, Siena

Oratorio di San Bernardino

Adjacent to the Basilica di San Francesco, the Oratorio di San Bernardino is located about a 10-minute walk from Siena's Duomo. This 15th-century chapel stands on the site where the Franciscan preacher San Bernardino of Siena frequently delivered sermons. The Oratorio is part of the Acropoli pass, which includes several significant churches. Inside, the ground floor exhibits a collection of paintings ranging from the 13th to the 19th centuries, sourced from various churches within the Siena diocese, and housed within the Diocesan Museum. The ceiling, adorned with 16th-century frescoes depicting a starry sky, adds to the space's grandeur.

The upper floor showcases invaluable religious artworks by Sano di Pietro, Pietro Lorenzetti, and Jacopo della Quercia. The chapel, however, is the main attraction with its walls covered in exquisite 16th-century frescoes by artists including Sodoma, Domenico Beccafumi, and Girolamo del Pacchia, illustrating scenes from the Virgin Mary's life and various saints. Address: Piazza San Francesco, Siena Website: (www.oratoriosanbernardino.siena.it)

Palazzo Salimbeni

Dominating Piazza Salimbeni, the 14th-century Gothic Palazzo Salimbeni is flanked by two other historic buildings. Originally, this piazza served as the palace's private garden, but by the mid-1800s, it was transformed into a public square, and the Palazzo Salimbeni underwent a significant renovation to align with the Neo-Gothic architectural trends of the time. Today, the building houses the headquarters of Monte dei Paschi di Siena, one of Italy's oldest banks, established in 1472.

The bank's art collections are not generally accessible to the public. Adjacent to Palazzo Salimbeni is the Palazzo Spannocchi, designed by architect Giuliano da Maiano for Ambrogio Spannocchi, who served as Treasurer to Pope Pius II. This Renaissance palace features loggias added in 1880 by Giuseppe Partini, who also contributed to the creation of the piazza and the renovation of Palazzo Salimbeni. Address: Piazza Salimbeni, Siena

Where to Eat

L'oro Di Siena

L'oro Di Siena, located at Via Giuseppe Garibaldi, 61, offers a cozy, intimate atmosphere with top-notch service. Enjoy award-winning Pecorino cheese, homemade Pappardelle with Rabbit, and Tuscan Pork, all made with fresh, local ingredients. Website: https://www.orodisiena.it/

Ristorante Campo Cedro

At Via Pian D'Ovile, 54, Ristorante Campo Cedro boasts creative dishes served under vaulted brick ceilings. Indulge in prawns with tartar sauce and saffron puffed rice, and Taglioni with Squid and Taggiasca olives, all prepared with meticulous care. Website: https://www.campocedro.com/

La Taverna Di San Giuseppe

Situated at Via Giovanni Duprè, 132, La Taverna Di San Giuseppe is set in an ancient Etruscan house. Sample historical Tuscan dishes like Malfatti Casalinghi and Tagliata, with local truffle, in a restaurant listed in the Michelin Guide since 2007. Website: http://tavernasangiuseppe.it/

Fischi Per Fiaschi

Fischi Per Fiaschi, at Via S. Marco, 43, offers a relaxed atmosphere with communal tables and affordable wines. Enjoy their Artichoke Rigatoni or Rib and Chickpeas Pasta, ideal for a light or hearty meal. Website: http://www.facebook.com/FischiXFiaschi

PARTICOLARE Di Siena

PARTICOLARE Di Siena, located at Via Baldassarre Peruzzi, 26, features inventive Tuscan dishes in a modern setting. The Up and Down Senesi Hills Tasting Menu, including Roe Deer and Venison, showcases their unique fusion of traditional and contemporary flavors. Website: http://www.particolaredisiena.com/

Ristorante Havana Club Siena

Ristorante Havana Club Siena, at Piazza Maestri del Lavoro, 27, provides a vibrant Cuban dining experience with large portions and live music. Savor a variety of meats and a buffet with rice and beans, served with flair. Website: https://www.facebook.com/HavanaClubSiena

Zest Ristorante & Wine Bar

Zest Ristorante & Wine Bar, at Costa Sant'Antonio, 13, offers excellent wine pairings with small plates in a cozy setting. Enjoy dishes like Homemade Ravioli Caprese and fried Squid, complemented by recommended wines like Roman Primitivo and Ghiaiolo. Contact +39 0577 47139 for more details.

Tre Cristi Enoteca Ristorante

Tre Cristi Enoteca Ristorante, located at Vicolo di Provenzano, 1/7, excels in seafood with its traditional ambiance. Opt for the Clamari with Monkfish instead of the heavy Spaghettoni to enjoy a fresh, balanced meal. Visit http://www.trecristi.com/ for more information.

Antica Trattoria Papei

Antica Trattoria Papei, at Piazza Mercato, 6, has been serving traditional dishes since 1939. Enjoy classic recipes like Tagliolini in Rabbit Sauce and Pheasant with Raisins, all while taking in views of historic architecture. Visit http://www.anticatrattoriapapei.com/ for more information.

Rome

Traveling from Pisa to Rome is straightforward, given the well-established connections by both air and land.

By Plane

The main gateway for flights from Pisa to Rome is Leonardo da Vinci Airport, also known as Fiumicino Airport, situated about 30 kilometers southwest of Rome's center. Passengers can access central Rome via two train services running every 30 minutes or buses operating on a similar schedule. The flight covers the 265 kilometers between Pisa and Rome in roughly 30 minutes, making it an efficient choice for travelers.

Fiumicino Airport primarily serves domestic flights from Terminal A and both domestic and international flights from Terminal B. Alternatively, Ciampino Airport, located 15 kilometers south of Rome, handles charter and European flights.

By Bus

Traveling from Pisa to Rome by bus is well-supported due to the popularity of both cities. Buses depart from Piazza Vittorio Emanuele II in Pisa and typically arrive at Stazione Terminale in Rome. Despite the convenience, many travelers prefer trains for this route due to their speed and comfort.

By Train

The train is a favored option for traveling between Pisa and Rome, offering a scenic and cost-effective journey. Approximately 20 trains run daily from Pisa's Central Station to Rome's Stazione Centrale, with travel times ranging from 3 to 4 hours. Tickets are reasonably priced, making it a popular choice.

By Car

For those who prefer a flexible travel experience, driving from Pisa to Rome is an option. Travelers should take the E80 expressway and then switch to the A12 Rome-Civitavecchia highway to reach Rome.

Top Things to Do in Rome

Colosseum (Colosseo)

Opened in A.D. 80, the Colosseum, an ancient Roman amphitheater, could accommodate about 50,000 spectators and is renowned for its engineering marvel and historical significance. It hosted gladiatorial contests and wild animal battles, marking it as both a site of brutal spectacles and architectural innovation. Today, it stands as one of the world's most iconic landmarks. The Colosseum is accessible via the Colosseo metro stop and is open daily from approximately 8:30 or 9 a.m. until 4:30 to 7 p.m., depending on the season. To skip long queues, purchase tickets online in advance for €18 (around $19.50) for adults, including same-day entry to the Roman Forum and Palatine Hill. Discounts are available for children, and guided tours may cost more.

Vatican Museums and Sistine Chapel

The Vatican Museums house some of the finest artworks in history and are among Rome's busiest attractions. To avoid the crowds, consider booking an early morning tour or checking for late opening hours. The Vatican City, the center of the Roman Catholic Church, is a significant destination encompassing the Sistine Chapel, St. Peter's Basilica, and the Museums. Guided tours are recommended due to the size and popularity of the site, though self-guided visits are also possible, typically requiring at least half a day. You must cover their knees and shoulders; shorts, short skirts, and sleeveless tops are not permitted. Suitable attire includes dresses that fall below the knee and long pants with a T-shirt.

Adult tickets start at €20 (approximately $21.60), while tickets for children aged 7 to 18 are €8 (about $8.66). Children under 6 enter for free. Audio guides cost €7 (about $7.50) if booked online in advance, or €8 at the door.

The museums are free on the last Sunday of each month but can be exceptionally crowded. The Vatican Museums are open Monday to Saturday from 8 a.m. to 7 p.m., with the last entry at 5 p.m. On the last Sunday of each month, they are open from 9 a.m. to 2 p.m., with the last entry at 12:30 p.m. The nearest Metro station is Ottaviano on Line A. Several bus lines also stop close to the museum entrance. The Vatican may close on certain days, including Christmas, so check the official [Vatican Museums website](http://www.museivaticani.va) for the latest information and any temporary closures.

St. Peter's Basilica (Basilica di San Pietro)

St. Peter's Basilica, the heart of Roman Catholicism located in Vatican City, is renowned for its architectural splendor and is open to the public daily without an entrance fee. However, it closes on Wednesday mornings for the Pope's audience. For an additional fee, you can climb to the dome's summit: 8 euros (approximately $8.65) for 551 steps or 10 euros (about $10.80) for an elevator ride to a terrace, followed by 320 steps. The panoramic view of Rome is spectacular.

If you wish to see the Pope, attend the Wednesday General Audience in St. Peter's Square, which is free but requires advance tickets. No ticket is needed to see the Pope on Sundays at noon in St. Peter's Square.

Note the strict dress code: shoulders and knees must be covered, and tattoos should be concealed. Daily Mass services are held, and expect long queues, though they move quickly. For more details on tours and visiting tips, consult the [official Vatican website](http://www.vatican.va). Open daily from 7 a.m. to 7 p.m. The dome is accessible from 7:30 a.m., closing at 5 p.m. in winter and 6 p.m. in summer. Entry to the basilica is free; fees apply only for dome access. Take Metro Line A (red) to Ottaviano station.

Roman Forum

Adjacent to the Colosseum, the Roman Forum provides a glimpse into Ancient Rome's historic core, featuring remains of significant structures like the Arch of Septimius Severus, the Temple of Saturn, and the Arch of Titus. Though largely in ruins, the site offers a rich historical context. I recommend renting an audio guide or joining a guided tour due to the lack of detailed informational plaques.

Plan for ample time to explore the ruins and dress appropriately for the weather as there is minimal shade.

Open daily at 9 a.m., with closing times varying by season. Entrance costs 18 euros (about $19.50) for a self-guided visit, which includes access to the Colosseum and Palatine Hill.

Discounted tickets are available for children, and admission is covered with a Roma Pass. Guided tours are priced separately. The nearest metro station is Colosseo. For more information, visit the [official Roman Forum website](http://www.coopculture.it).

Trevi Fountain (Fontana di Trevi)

The Trevi Fountain, located in the bustling Trevi district among hotels, shops, and nightlife, is a baroque masterpiece completed in the 1750s. This iconic structure features Oceanus, the sea god, emerging from the fountain, accompanied by Tritons. Legend suggests that tossing one, two, or three coins into the fountain—using your right hand over your left shoulder—guarantees a return to Rome, falling in love with a Roman, and marrying them. The coins collected are donated to local charities. The fountain is beautifully illuminated at night, making it a popular spot for evening visits, though it can be crowded with tourists and street vendors. The Trevi Fountain is located near the Barberini metro stop, approximately a 10-minute walk east of the Pantheon. The fountain is accessible 24/7 and free to visit. If you join a guided tour, it will likely include a stop at the Trevi Fountain.

Pantheon

The Pantheon, originally a Roman temple now functioning as a church, stands as a marvel of ancient architecture with its impressive proportions, completed around A.D. 120. The Pantheon also serves as the final resting place for notable figures such as the artist Raphael and Italian kings Victor Emmanuel II and Umberto I. You can enjoy exploring the nearby Piazza della Rotonda, which is ideal for coffee, pizza, or gelato. For a deeper understanding of its history, consider a guided tour. Early morning visits can help avoid crowds. The Pantheon is located at the corner of Navona and Campo, accessible via the Barberini metro stop. Open daily from 9 a.m. to 7 p.m., with the last entry at 6:45 p.m. General admission is 5 euros (about $5.50) for adults, free for children 17 and younger. Audio guide tickets cost 15 euros (around $16) for adults and 10 euros (approximately $11) for children 17 and younger. For more information, visit the [Pantheon website](http://www.pantheonroma.com).

Piazza Navona

Piazza Navona is a historic square in Rome, renowned for its vibrant atmosphere and lively street performers. Surrounded by cafes and shops, which some visitors find pricey, the square is famous for its impressive Baroque architecture and monuments. Key highlights include Gian Lorenzo Bernini's "Fountain of the Four Rivers" and Francesco Borromini's "Sant'Agnese in Agone." To reach Piazza Navona, take Metro Line A (red) to Barberini station and walk approximately one mile west. The square is open for visitors at all hours, and entry is free.

Fontana dei Quattro Fiumi

The Fontana dei Quattro Fiumi, or Fountain of the Four Rivers, is the central feature of Piazza Navona. Designed by Gian Lorenzo Bernini, this fountain showcases four figures symbolizing major rivers known in the 17th century: the Ganges

(Asia), the Danube (Europe), the Nile (Africa), and the Río de la Plata (Americas). Each figure is adorned with animals, plants, and other symbols to reflect their respective regions. Located in the middle of Piazza Navona, the fountain is easily accessible from the square and is open for viewing at any time. Entry to see the fountain is free. Take from the Pantheon, it's about a four-minute walk west to Piazza Navona.

Spanish Steps (Piazza di Spagna)

Located in Piazza di Spagna, the Spanish Steps are a renowned landmark named after the nearby Spanish Embassy. These steps, which connect the Piazza di Spagna with the Trinità dei Monti church, are notable for their historical significance and picturesque setting. The steps are particularly charming in spring when adorned with blooming azaleas. Despite mixed opinions, the panoramic views from the top of the 135 steps are widely appreciated. The Spanish Steps are accessible 24/7, and there is no admission fee. The nearest metro station is Spagna, just a short walk away.

Piazza del Popolo

Piazza del Popolo, a central square in Rome, is notable for its striking architecture and historical significance. Established in the mid-1500s, it serves as a major intersection for Via di Ripetta, Via del Corso, and Via del Babuino.

At its center stands the Flaminio Obelisk, originally erected in Egypt around 1300 B.C. and relocated to Rome by Emperor Augustus. The obelisk, which measures nearly 120 feet including its base and cross, is a focal point of the piazza. Surrounding the square are several important sites, including the Chiesa di Santa Maria del Popolo and its twin church, Santa Maria in Montesanto. These churches feature impressive artworks and architectural details. Piazza del Popolo is open 24/7, though the churches have specific visiting hours. The closest metro stop is Flaminio, located across from the west side of Villa Borghese.

Galleria Borghese

The Galleria Borghese, housed in a 17th-century villa commissioned by Cardinal Scipione Borghese, is a prominent art museum in Rome renowned for its impressive collection and beautiful gardens. Originally intended to display Cardinal Borghese's extensive art collection, the museum now features masterpieces by renowned artists. Highlights include Canova's "Venus Victrix," Bernini's sculptures "David" and "Apollo and Daphne," and Caravaggio's "Boy with a Basket of Fruit" and "David with the Head of Goliath."

The museum limits its visitor count to 360 per session, ensuring an intimate viewing experience of its notable artworks. During your visit, keep your ticket handy as it is required for restroom access.   Open from 9 a.m. to 7 p.m., Tuesday through Sunday. Closed on Mondays. Admission is 13 euros (approximately $14) for adults, 2 euros (around $2) for students aged 18 to 25, and free for children aged 17 and under, although a 2-euro booking fee per child applies. Each ticket includes a designated entry and exit time; plan to arrive 30 minutes early. Visits are limited to two-hour sessions, and tickets must be booked in advance. The Roma Pass covers admission, but booking is still necessary. Website: (https://www.galleriaborghese.beniculturali.it). Accessible from the Spagna metro stop, with additional bus routes servicing the area.

Campo de' Fiori

Campo de' Fiori, a lively square in Rome, offers a dynamic experience both during the day and at night. By day, it transforms into a bustling market filled with fresh produce, flowers, and local vendors, while its evening ambiance shifts to a vibrant nightlife scene with numerous bars and eateries. Although the square has retained much of its early 19th-century charm, it is now surrounded by modern pizzerias, cafes, and gelaterias. You can enjoy observing the bustling market atmosphere and the lively bar scene. For those who appreciate architecture, the square's historical appeal alone makes it worth a visit. South of Piazza Navona. The area is open 24/7. For those not walking or biking, buses provide convenient access.

Church of St. Louis of the French

The Church of St. Louis of the French (San Luigi dei Francesi), located near Piazza Navona, is a must-see for art enthusiasts, particularly those interested in Caravaggio. Inside, you can view three significant works by the renowned Baroque painter: "The Calling of St. Matthew," "Saint Matthew and the Angel," and "The Martyrdom of Saint Matthew." To enhance your visit, it is advisable to read about these masterpieces beforehand, as the church does not provide information on-site. However, a prerecorded audio tour can be accessed by scanning a QR code available within the church. Open daily from 9:30 a.m. to 6:30 p.m., with a lunch break from 12:15 p.m. to 2:30 p.m. Note that the church may close temporarily for prayer or services. Website: [Church of St. Louis of the French](https://www.sanluigidifrancesi.com)

Capitoline Museums (Musei Capitolini)

The Capitoline Museums, established in the 15th century, are located in Piazza del Campidoglio, just north of the Colosseum and Roman Forum. This renowned museum houses the iconic bronze statue of the Capitoline She-wolf, which, according to legend, nursed the twin founders of Rome, Romulus and Remus. The museum's collection includes Roman busts, notable statues such as the equestrian Marcus Aurelius, and artworks by Caravaggio and Battista. Additionally, the museums offer impressive views of the Roman Forum. You should take note of the elaborate ceilings and consider exploring beyond the primary exhibits, despite some critiques about the museum's layout and staff demeanor. Open daily from 9:30 a.m. to 7:30 p.m. General admission is 18.50 euros (approximately $20). Children aged 6 and under can enter for free. Video guides are available for an extra 7 euros (about $7.50), and audio guides for children in Italian, French, and English cost 5 euros (around $5). Admission is included with the Roma Pass. For further details, visit the [Capitoline Museums website](https://museicapitolini.org).

Trastevere

Trastevere, located southeast of Vatican City, offers a glimpse into authentic Roman life. This charming neighborhood is renowned for its cobblestone streets and narrow alleys, housing the Basilica of Santa Maria in Trastevere, numerous local eateries, and boutique shops. Trastevere's ambiance is often compared to New York's Greenwich Village or Paris's Left Bank, making it a favored spot for visitors seeking a more genuine Roman experience away from the city center. The area is ideal for exploring on foot, though tram No. 8 provides convenient access. Local tours, particularly those focusing on culinary experiences, are available for a deeper dive into Trastevere's culture. Walk from the city center or take tram No. 8.

Santa Maria della Vittoria

Santa Maria della Vittoria, featured prominently in Dan Brown's novel Angels & Demons, attracts numerous visitors, especially fans of the book. Despite the crowds, art enthusiasts are drawn to the church's Cornaro Chapel, renowned for Gian Lorenzo Bernini's Ecstasy of Saint Teresa sculpture. This Baroque masterpiece, acclaimed for its intricate details, is a highlight for many. The church, located a short five-minute walk north of the Repubblica metro station and less than a mile south of the Galleria Borghese, is smaller compared to other major Roman sites, so expect tight quarters during peak tourist times. It is also noted for having irregular opening hours, which can be checked on the church's [website](https://www.santamariadellavittoria.it).

Open daily from 8:30 a.m. to noon and 4 p.m. to 6 p.m. Visits are not permitted during Mass.

Museo Nazionale di Castel Sant'Angelo

Originally built as Emperor Hadrian's mausoleum, Castel Sant'Angelo has served multiple roles including a papal fortress, military barracks, and prison. It now functions as a museum that highlights both its military history and the remarkable frescoes added when it was used as a residence. Appreciate the museum for its rich historical exhibits and, notably, the panoramic views from the top terrace, known as the Terrace of the Angel, which offers spectacular vistas of Rome. Open Tuesday to Sunday from 9 a.m. to 7:30 p.m., with the last entry at 6:30 p.m. Admission is 16 euros (approximately $17) for adults, while children under 18 enter free. Roma Pass holders receive complimentary entry. For additional details, visit the [Museo Nazionale di Castel Sant'Angelo's website](https://castelsantangelo.beniculturali.it).

Basilica di San Clemente

The Basilica di San Clemente, located just a short walk east of the Colosseum, is a historical marvel that reveals multiple layers of Roman history. The structure comprises a 12th-century church built on top of a 4th-century church, which itself was constructed over a 2nd-century pagan temple. You can descend through these layers to uncover a shrine dedicated to Mithras, a deity popular in the 2nd and 3rd centuries. The original building is believed to have been an ancient mint.

The site, which offers a fascinating historical narrative, operates daily with visiting hours from 9 a.m. to 12:30 p.m. and 2 p.m. to 6 p.m. from Monday to Saturday, and from noon to 6 p.m. on Sundays. Note that the last entry is 30 minutes before closing. While entry to the church is free, access to the lower levels requires a fee: 10 euros (approximately $11) for adults and 5 euros (about $5) for students up to age 26. Children under 16 enter for free when accompanied by an adult. Be cautious of panhandlers around the church; some may falsely claim to represent the church and ask for donations to allow entry. For further details, visit the [Basilica di San Clemente's website](https://basilicasanclemente.com).

Appian Way

The Ancient Appian Way (Via Appia Antica), one of Rome's oldest roads, dates back to 312 B.C. It is renowned for historic sites such as the tomb of Caecilia Metella and the location of Spartacus' execution in 71 B.C. Stretching 38.5 miles, the most notable section runs through Parco dell'Appia Antica, approximately 2 miles south of the Colosseum. Wear comfortable walking shoes and carry water, as the path can be lengthy and exposed. The area is best visited during the day to avoid less secure areas at night. Access to the Appian Way and the park is free. To reach the site, take bus No. 118 from outside Porta San Sebastiano.

Colle del Gianicolo

Colle del Gianicolo, also known as Janiculum Hill, offers a rewarding hike with sweeping panoramic views of Rome. Located west of the Tiber River near Trastevere, this elevated spot provides a striking perspective of the city, including landmarks such as St. Peter's Basilica and the Altare della Patria. Despite its prominent position, Janiculum Hill is not one of Rome's traditional seven hills, as it lies outside the ancient city boundaries. In addition to the views, visitors can admire historical monuments like the Fontana dell'Acqua Paola, or Il Fontanone, originally constructed in the early 1600s.

I recommend visits at sunrise or sunset for the most stunning scenery. While it may not be essential for first-time tourists, it offers a peaceful escape from Rome's busier areas. The hill is accessible via paths in Gianicolo Park and is open around the clock with no admission fee.

Palazzo Doria Pamphilj

Situated on the lively Via del Corso, the Palazzo Doria Pamphilj is a gem of aristocratic architecture that contrasts with the bustling city outside. Upon entering, you are greeted by a serene courtyard, leading to a hall of mirrors reminiscent of the one at Versailles, adorned with Venetian mirrors, antique statues, and chandeliers. Dating back to the 16th century, the palace's gallery, renovated in the 18th century, houses the Doria Pamphilj family's private art collection, featuring works by Raphael and Caravaggio. Notably, the Velázquez Cabinet contains a marble bust of Pope Innocent X by Gian Lorenzo Bernini and a portrait by Velázquez.

For an additional fee, you can explore the "secret apartment," believed to be occasionally used by the princess, offering a glimpse into the family's personal belongings and furnishings. This intimate experience provides a unique perspective, akin to scenes from Paolo Sorrentino's film "La Grande Bellezza." Despite its central location, the palace is noted for its relative tranquility and low tourist traffic. The gallery is open Monday to Thursday from 9 a.m. to 7 p.m., and Friday to Sunday from 10 a.m. to 8 p.m. It is closed on the third Wednesday of each month and select holidays.

Admission is 16 euros (approximately $17) for adults, while children 12 and under enter for free. Audio guides in English are included with the ticket. For more information, visit the [official website](https://www.doriapamphilj.it).

Jewish Ghetto

The Jewish Ghetto, nestled between the Tiber River and Campo de' Fiori, represents Rome's historic Jewish community, the oldest in Europe. Established by a papal decree in 1555, this walled-off area restricted Jewish professions until its removal in 1888. To delve into its rich history, visit the Jewish Museum of Rome, which is housed within the Great Synagogue. The museum features religious artifacts and detailed historical exhibits. Admission includes a guided tour of the Great Synagogue, the only opportunity to explore its ornate interiors without attending a religious service.

The neighborhood is vibrant with numerous restaurants, shops, and bakeries. For a culinary treat, try carciofi alla giudea (fried artichokes) at a local eatery or sample crostata di ricotta e visciole (ricotta and cherry pie) from Forno Boccione. Nearby, the Fontana delle Tartarughe, a Renaissance-era fountain with turtle statues, is also worth a visit.

The neighborhood is accessible around the clock at no cost. However, the museum requires a ticket priced at 11 euros (approximately $12) for adults, while children aged 10 and under enter for free. The museum operates from Sunday to Thursday, with varying hours from 10 a.m. to 4 p.m., 4:30 p.m., 5 p.m., or 7 p.m. depending on the month. On Fridays, it is open from 9 a.m. to 2 p.m., with the last entry typically 45 minutes before closing. For detailed information, visit the [official website](https://www.mejudaism.it).

MAXXI

MAXXI, the National Museum of 21st Century Art, offers a contemporary contrast to Rome's ancient and Baroque art. Located in the Flaminio neighborhood north of Piazza del Popolo, this museum is the creation of Iraqi-British architect Zaha Hadid, renowned for its striking modern architecture featuring sweeping lines, floating steel staircases, and glass ceilings. The museum houses over 400 artworks by Italian and international artists, including Andy Warhol, Francesco

Clemente, and Gerhard Richter, and features a range of media from photography and film to art installations and performance pieces.

Before visiting, check the museum's current exhibitions, as past shows have included Bob Dylan's videos, Italian filmmaker Pier Paolo Pasolini's works, and mid-century modern architecture by Lina Bo Bardi. MAXXI also occasionally hosts off-site exhibitions and guided tours of Casa Balla, the studio of futurist artist Giacomo Balla. MAXXI is open from Tuesday to Sunday, 11 a.m. to 7 p.m. Admission is 15 euros (about $16) for adults, with free entry for visitors aged 17 and under. Booking tickets online in advance can save you one euro. For more details, visit the [official website](https://www.maxxi.art).

Mercato di Testaccio

For an authentic Roman market experience away from the typical tourist spots, head to Mercato di Testaccio.

This expansive covered market, situated in the Testaccio neighborhood across the Tiber River from Trastevere, serves as a bustling hub for local shopping. It features a variety of stalls offering fresh fruits, vegetables, fish, and meats. Among the highlights are food stalls where you can grab prepared meals. At

Casa Manco, order pizza al taglio by the slice to sample various toppings. For sandwiches, Mordi e Vai is a must-visit; this small stall specializes in sandwiches made from traditional Roman offcuts, integral to the local quinto quarto cuisine. Testaccio, historically known for its slaughterhouse, is the birthplace of recipes utilizing less popular meat cuts, such as trippa alla romana (tripe in tomato sauce) and coda alla vaccinara (oxtail stew). Mordi e Vai also offers vegetarian options. Mercato di Testaccio is open Monday through Saturday from 7 a.m. to 3:30 p.m. Admission to the market is free. For further details, visit the [official website](https://www.mercatoditestaccio.it).

Where To Eat

Love Specialty Croissants

Located a few blocks north of the Vatican Museums, Love Specialty Croissants offers a selection of French- and Italian-style pastries, both savory and sweet, alongside single-origin coffee from Aliena Coffee Roasters. Highlights include the Moon Love, a coffee cream-filled, flaky pastry topped with coffee crumble. Find it at Via Tunisi 51, 00192 Roma RM.

Orma Roma

Chef Roy Caceres's Orma, near the Galleria Borghese, features a bistrot, cocktail bar, and restaurant blending Colombian and Italian flavors. Signature dishes include Uovo 65° Carbonara and lacquered eel with pickled onions. Located at Via Boncompagni, 31/33, 00187 Roma RM, Italy, call 06 854 3182.

Bonci Pizzarium

Near the Vatican Museums, Bonci Pizzarium is renowned for its pizza al taglio, featuring cold-fermented, heirloom wheat dough with biodynamic toppings. Signatures like tomato-oregano and potato-mozzarella are usually available. Located at Via della Meloria 43, 00136 Roma Lazio, call 06 3974 5416.

Tianci Chongqing Farm Hot Pot

Close to the Spanish Steps and Trevi Fountain, Tianci Chongqing Farm Hot Pot offers spicy broth cauldrons for cooking various ingredients. Located at Via Barberini, 53/55/57, 00187 Roma RM, Italy, call 06 594 3809.

Colline Emiliane

Near the Trevi Fountain, this trattoria offers Emilia-Romagna dishes like house-made tortelli di zucca and tagliatelle alla bolognese.

Enjoy mains such as bollito misto and fried liver. Located at Via degli Avignonesi 22, 00187 Roma Lazio, call 06 481 7538.

Armando al Pantheon

Steps from the Pantheon, this family-run restaurant serves Roman classics like fettuccine con le rigaglie di pollo and coda alla vaccinara. Seasonal dishes include puntarelle and carciofi alla romana. Located at Salita dè Crescenzi 31, 00186 Roma Lazio, call 06 6880 3034. **Supplizio**

Chef Arcangelo Dandini's casual spot serves fried Roman street food like suppli, crocchette di patate, and crema fritta. Located in central Rome at Via dei Banchi Vecchi 143, 00186 Roma Lazio, call 06 8987 1920.

Cesare Al Pellegrino

Near Campo dei Fiori, this resurrected trattoria offers a succinct menu including romanesco and skate soup and pan-fried meatballs. Located at Via del Pellegrino 117, 00186 Roma Lazio, call 06 6880 1978.

Hosteria Grappolo d'Oro

Known for friendly service, this restaurant serves Roman classics like tonnarelli cacio e pepe and roasted suckling lamb.

The five-course tasting menu is 34 euros. Located at Piazza della Cancelleria 80, 00186 Roma Lazio, call 06 689 7080.

Forno Campo de' Fiori

Forno Campo de' Fiori offers sweet and savory Roman treats like jam tarts and pizza alla pala. Located at Piazza Campo de' Fiori 22, 00186 Roma, call 06 6880 6662.

Mazzo

Mazzo, run by Francesca Barreca and Marco Baccanelli, serves nostalgic dishes like wagon wheel pasta with braised beef and fried tripe.

Located at Via degli Equi 62, 00185 Roma Lazio, call 06 6942 0455.

Pasticceria Regoli

Pasticceria Regoli, established in 1916, offers cakes, maritozzi, and seasonal treats. Located at Via Dello Statuto 60, 00185 Roma Lazio, call 06 487 2812.

Enqutatash

Enqutatash, near Via Prenestina, serves Ethiopian and Eritrean dishes with house-made injera. Located at Viale della Stazione Prenestina 55, 00177 Roma Lazio, call 06 273767.

Salumeria Roscioli

Salumeria Roscioli, a deli, wine bar, and restaurant, offers standout cheeses, cured meats, and pasta. Located at Via dei Giubbonari 21, 00186 Roma, call 06 687 5287.

Beppe e I Suoi Formaggi

Beppe e I Suoi Formaggi offers a curated selection of Italian and French cheeses and wines. Located at 9A Via di S. Maria del Pianto, 00186 Lazio, call 06 6819 2210.

Casalino Osteria Kosher

Casalino serves kosher dishes inspired by Rome's Jewish ghetto traditions, including deep-fried artichokes and modern twists like tuna carbonara. Located at Via del Portico d'Ottavia 1e, 00186 Roma, call 06 7978 1514.

Boccione – Il Forno del Ghetto

Boccione bakery, over three centuries old, offers specialties like pizza ebraica and ricotta sour-cherry tart. Located at Via del Portico d'Ottavia 1 (Piazza Costaguti), 00186 Roma, call 06 687 8637.

CHAPTER 9
TRAVEL RESOURCES FOR PISA

Travel Phrases

Greetings

- Hello: Ciao
- Good morning: Buongiorno
- Good afternoon: Buon pomeriggio
- Good evening: Buonasera
- Good night: Buonanotte
- Goodbye: Arrivederci
- Please: Per favore
- Thank you: Grazie
- You're welcome: Prego
- Excuse me: Mi scusi
- Yes: Sì
- No: No

Transportation Phrases

- Where is the bus stop?: Dov'è la fermata dell'autobus?
- I need a taxi: Ho bisogno di un taxi

- How much is a ticket to...?: Quanto costa un biglietto per...?
- Can you take me to...?: Può portarmi a...?
- Where is the train station?: Dov'è la stazione ferroviaria?
- Is this the right train/bus for...?: È questo il treno/l'autobus giusto per...?

Security Phrases**

- Help!: Aiuto!
- I am lost: Mi sono perso/a
- Call the police: Chiama la polizia
- Where is the nearest police station?: Dov'è la stazione di polizia più vicina?
- I need help: Ho bisogno di aiuto

In a Hotel

- I have a reservation: Ho una prenotazione
- Do you have a room available?: Avete una camera disponibile?
- What is the Wi-Fi password?: Qual è la password del Wi-Fi?
- I would like to check out: Vorrei fare il check-out
- Can I get a wake-up call?: Posso avere una sveglia?

In Restaurants

- A table for two, please: Un tavolo per due, per favore
- Can I see the menu?: Posso vedere il menu?
- I am vegetarian: Sono vegetariano/a
- The bill, please: Il conto, per favore
- What do you recommend?: Cosa mi consiglia?

Time

- What time is it?: Che ore sono?
- It's 8 o'clock: Sono le otto
- Morning: Mattina
- Afternoon: Pomeriggio
- Evening: Sera
- Night: Notte

Numbers (0-10)

- 0: Zero
- 1: Uno
- 2: Due
- 3: Tre
- 4: Quattro
- 5: Cinque
- 6: Sei

- 7: Sette
- 8: Otto
- 9: Nove
- 10: Dieci

Shopping Phrases

- How much does this cost?: Quanto costa questo?
- Do you accept credit cards?: Accettate carte di credito?
- Can I try this on?: Posso provarlo/a?
- Do you have this in a different size?: Avete questo in un'altra taglia?
- Where is the fitting room?: Dov'è il camerino?

Emergency Phrases

- I need a doctor: Ho bisogno di un dottore
- Call an ambulance: Chiama un'ambulanza
- Where is the nearest hospital?: Dov'è l'ospedale più vicino?
- I am allergic to...: Sono allergico/a a...
- I need a pharmacy: Ho bisogno di una farmacia

Sightseeing

- Where is the Leaning Tower?: Dov'è la Torre Pendente?

- Is there a guided tour?: C'è una visita guidata?
- How much is the entrance fee?: Quanto costa l'ingresso?
- What time does it open/close?: A che ora apre/chiude?
- Can I take photos here?: Posso fare foto qui?

Asking for Help

- Can you help me?: Può aiutarmi?
- I need directions to...: Ho bisogno di indicazioni per...
- Do you speak English?: Parla inglese?
- Can you repeat that, please?: Può ripetere, per favore?
- Where can I find...?: Dove posso trovare...?

Tourist Information Centers

The Province of Pisa, including the city of Pisa, has about 20 tourist information offices to assist visitors. These offices are spread across various areas: three in Monti Pisani, four in Valdarno, six in Valdera and Colline Pisane, and two in Val di Cecina. In the city of Pisa itself, there are several offices to ensure tourists have a smooth experience from the start. The main tourist office is located in the Piazza dei Miracoli, while others can be found at the Galileo Galilei Airport and Piazza Vittorio Emanuele.

Field of Miracles Tourist Information

The central tourist office, located in the Field of Miracles, is the main hub for visitors due to its proximity to Pisa's most famous landmarks. This office can be found at Piazza Arcivescovado 8, Pisa, Italy, and is open daily from 10:00 AM to 7:00 PM. Contact them at 0039 (0)50 42291 or via fax at 0039 (0)50 504 067. They offer services in Italian, English, German, French, and Spanish.

Pisa Airport Tourist Information

Located in the arrivals hall of Galileo Galilei Airport, this office serves as the primary point of contact for many visitors entering Pisa. The address is Galileo Galilei Airport, Pisa, Italy, and it is open daily from 11:00 AM to 11:00 PM. You can reach them at 0039 (0)50 502 518, and they provide assistance in English, German, French, and Spanish.

Train Station Tourist Information Office

Another important office is situated near the central train station at Piazza Vittorio Emanuele II, 16, Pisa, Italy. Though it has shorter hours, it remains a valuable resource for travelers. It operates Monday to Friday from 9:00 AM to 7:00 PM, and Saturday from 9:00 AM to 1:30 PM, but is closed on Sundays and public holidays.

Contact number is 0039 (0)50 42291, fax is 0039 (0)50 504 067, and languages spoken include English, French, German, and Spanish.

Ponte di Mezzo Tourist Information Office

This often overlooked office is located at Piazza XX Settembre, corner of Lungarno Galilei. It is open every day from 8:30 AM to 1:30 PM. Contact them at 0039 (0)50 910 350 or fax at 0039 (0)50 910 933. They offer services in English and French.

Emergency Contacts

For health emergencies, visitors in Pisa should go to Pisa Hospital located on Via Bonanno, or call 0039 (0)55 992 300. Another emergency number to call is 118. It is crucial for tourists to have up-to-date medical insurance to avoid complications. For minor health concerns, pharmacies provide an alternative.

In case of fire, the fire department can be reached at 115, and for other emergencies, the carabinieri can be contacted at 112. Additionally, the Office for the Protection of Tourists Rights is available to handle complaints and issues faced by tourists. This office is situated at Agenzia per il Turismo di Pisa, Via

Matteucci-Galleria Gerace 14, Pisa, and can be reached via fax at 0039 (0)50 929 764.

CONCLUSION

Thank you for choosing my guide to explore the wonders of Pisa. This enchanting city, with its iconic Leaning Tower, historic piazzas, and vibrant cultural scene, offers a unique blend of history, art, and modern charm. Whether you've marveled at the architecture in Piazza dei Miracoli, strolled along the Arno River, or savored authentic Tuscan cuisine, I hope this guide has enhanced your journey and helped you uncover the hidden gems that make Pisa so special.

I appreciate your trust in my work and your support for this book. It has been a joy to share my insights and experiences with you. May your time in Pisa be filled with unforgettable memories, delightful discoveries, and the warm hospitality of its people.

Buon viaggio and happy exploring!

Printed in Great Britain
by Amazon